T.E.WIGSTON 200

TEESSIDE
RAILWAYS
A VIEW FROM THE PAST

NORMAN HILL

Ian Allan
PUBLISHING

Contents

Front cover:
Coal Road crossing on the Barnard Castle to Bishop Auckland line was where single running track started despite the presence of two roads! On 23 August 1952 the first of two 'J25s' takes the tablet for this double-headed Kirkby Stephen to West Auckland goods, for permission to commence the climb towards Lands Viaduct. *J. W. Armstrong*

Back cover:
In January 1962, 'J27' No 65870 creates a typical Teesside scene as she eases a goods towards Dock Hill Junction and Middlesbrough from Newport. *Dr D. P. Williams/Ian Allan Library*

Title page:
The eastern frontier of the S&DR was extended in 1846 from Middlesbrough to Redcar and in 1861 onwards to Saltburn along the heavily graded Yorkshire coast. A half-hourly service ran between Middlesbrough and Saltburn and there were eventually through services to Whitby and Scarborough. Here, 'A8' 4-6-2T No 69854 sets out purposefully from Whitby for Middlesbrough via Battersby with the famous abbey in the background. Today, trains from Tyneside, Bishop Auckland and Darlington still run through Teesside to Saltburn. *A. M. Ross*

First published 2001

ISBN 0 7110 2803 6

© Ian Allan Publishing Ltd 2001

Published by Ian Allan Publishing — an imprint of Ian Allan Publishing Ltd, Riverdene Business Park, Molesey Road, Hersham, Surrey KT12 4RG
Printed by Ian Allan Printing Ltd, Riverdene Business Park, Molesey Road, Hersham, Surrey KT12 4RG

Code: 0111 / A3

Preface and Acknowledgements

The Stockton & Darlington is usually seen as the world's first railway, *Rocket* is frequently regarded as the world's first steam locomotive and George Stephenson is hailed as the world's first railway engineer. None of these 'firsts' was actually quite first in its particular field, and they all beg investigation in any study of North Eastern railways. In this all-too-brief study of Teesside's pioneering railways I have attempted to show these and similar early railway topics in their correct historical context, although controversy will always rage over some issues, notably over 'firsts' in the field of the steam locomotive.

Britain's Industrial Revolution was undoubtedly the first of its kind — a first which has ultimately proved to be detrimental to Britain, as other nations have found the time and the resources to build their own 'improved' industrial societies and so replace the British prototype upon which they were initially so dependent.

I have tried here to bring railways and history together in that small corner of North East England which played such a big part in the first act in the theatre of world industrialisation. In pursuit of this aim I have followed a classic trail which started inevitably with W. W. Tomlinson's historic *North Eastern Railway* and ended, by no means finally, with the multiple works of Ken Hoole, passing on the way such worthies as C. J. Allen, O. S. Nock and Professor Jack Simmons. However, my Bibliography also includes names not usually associated with railway history; Eric Hobsbawm, S. S. Checkland and J. Stevenson are just three of the many recent scholars who have discussed the social conditions of the Britain in which the first railways developed then declined. Our debt to them, however, is no greater than that which we owe to Allan Stobbs, Minnie Horton, Eveline Johnson and other local people who have set down their lifetime memories of Durham villages, Teesside town and country, and, indeed, of the proud North East. They have been bravely published by county and local district authorities.

Beyond the literary sources my own debt extends initially to Ian Allan Publishing and Peter Waller who gave me the chance to enter the ranks of railway writers. I also thank Terry Silcock at the RCTS library for his forbearance — and I promise I will return the books soon!

In the North I owe special thanks to archivist-librarian Ann Wilson for her assistance in the Ken Hoole Study Centre in Darlington's North Road Museum during my several essential visits. She was most helpful in supplying many of the photographs, all of which I have tried to acknowledge; if any have been missed I beg indulgence and point out their valuable contribution to history!

I am also grateful for advice from members of the North Eastern Railway Association, but most especially to Ken Appleby, whose own work has proved invaluable, who has saved me from a serious failure at Bowesfield Junction and is always keen to give me 'section clear'. John Wigston, whose splendid painting has been used on the endpapers, has also been more than helpful. I must not forget 'Jock' — and his sacrilegious praise for Oliver Bulleid — for showing me around Shildon and allowing me to 'footplate' *Sans Pareil*!

Finally, thanks are due to the patient family, always ready in the North to put me up at Sedgefield or Fishburn at a moment's notice, while in Hertfordshire my wife has endured two years during which books, maps and railway photos have gradually buried the dining-table, the rediscovery of which has now curtailed two years of teenage TV dinners!

Norman Hill
July 2001

Photographs credited to 'Darlington' are from the collection in The Ken Hoole Study Centre, Darlington Railway Centre & Museum, North Road Station, Darlington.

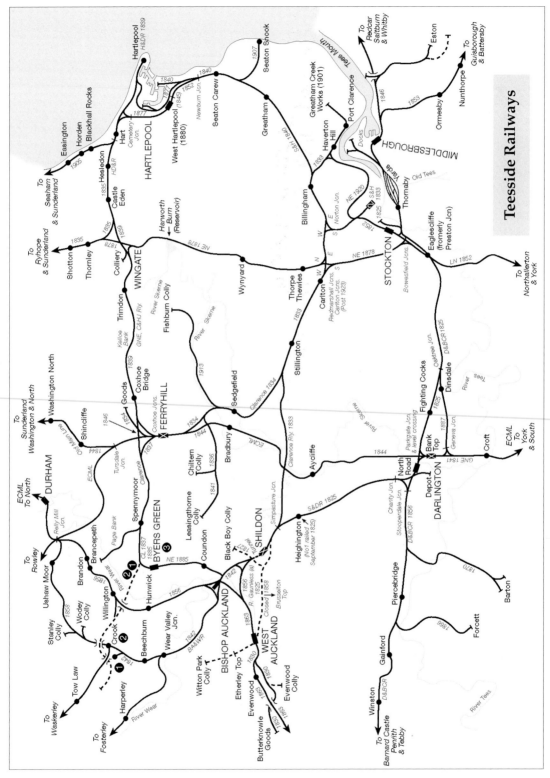

Teesside Railways

4

1. Three Railways

In 1815, a third of a million troops returned to Britain from the wars against Napoleon. They found the land's ancient trades and manufactures fast falling under the influence of the machine as Britain proceeded with the unique and peaceful revolution in industry which had been so rudely interrupted by the unique and bloody social revolution in France. In textiles, ironworking and mining, steam-driven machines played an increasingly important part. By the mid-18th century stationary steam engines were in use throughout the country but mainly in the North where the cotton industry had changed from a family home occupation into regimented mechanisation in the grim new mills and factories. The fertile lowlands of the South still relied mainly on agriculture, although field enclosure and new farming methods had driven labour increasingly from the land and into the new industrial towns where the 'factory system' bred incredible poverty and hardship among the 'labouring poor'. Further north, steadily increasing demand for coal from the new industries was met by new, deeper coal mines around which grew the pit settlements, the villages of a proud new race of workers — the miners.

By the early 19th century, most of the South's domestic coal was carried by sea in collier brigs from the ports of Wearside and Tyneside. The rivers serving these ports were quite close to the coal mines and coal had long been hauled between pit and river on wooden-railed wagonways. But, as coal production soared to meet the new industrial demand, it became evident that either many more horses would be needed or else a new and more powerful means of bulk haulage must be found. This situation was exacerbated by the shortage of horses, which were requisitioned to work and die in the wars. Mine owners looked at the great fixed steam hauling and pumping engines of Newcomen and Watt — members of another new race of industrial men, the engineers — and wondered whether this same power could be used to haul coals along the railways.

As a result of subsequent experiments, two independent colliery railways on Tyneside constructed steam locomotives which started in revenue-earning service in 1814. At Wylam Colliery, owner Christopher Blackett, with his colliery viewer, Thomas Hedley, and foreman smith, Timothy Hackworth, built a locomotive from the plans of Richard Trevithick's very first 'tram-engine' which had run at Pen-y-Darren ironworks in South Wales some 10 years earlier. Entrepreneurs Blackett and Trevithick most likely met while on business in London. Meanwhile, at nearby Killingworth an engine-winder named George Stephenson constructed a locomotive from ideas gained from spying activities at Wylam and at the neighbouring Kenton Colliery where two rack-rail locomotives were on loan from Middleton Colliery near Leeds. These were the completely independent invention of John Blenkinsop and Matthew Murray and worked successfully at Middleton for some 25 years. The Middleton Colliery Railway was undoubtedly the first revenue-earning steam-worked railway in the world.

Middleton's engineer Matthew Murray was a native of Stockton-on-Tees where his ingenuity might well have assisted the coal owners of southwest Durham in the solution of their own unique coal transport problem. They looked north with envy at the short wooden-railed wagonways which their northern neighbours had developed in order to despatch their coals directly to both Tyneside and Wearside loading staithes. Their own coals had to be carried 30 miles eastwards by the most treacherous roads and trackways to Stockton on the Tees before transport by ship could be contemplated through the long and tortuous navigation necessary to clear Teesmouth, again in inconvenient contrast to both Wearmouth and Tynemouth. As the demand for more coal escalated it became more and more obvious to the south Durham coal owners and their merchant colleagues that the old road route to the River Tees was woefully inadequate.

This problem of Teesside coal transport was originally addressed in 1768 when an engineer, Robert Whitworth, suggested a canal between Winston, south of the Auckland field, and Stockton. But this and various other ideas failed

Above:
Edward Pease is seen here at the height of his powers, the epitome of the new 19th century industrial aristocrat, rich beyond earlier commoners' dreams, proud, and very religious, the Peases being devout Quakers. They were a traditional land-owning family which combined, through marriage, with the expanding textile industry, and, through Edward's father's entrepreneurial foresight, in banking for fellow industrial capitalists. Edward's own interests branched out still further to include coal and mining. It is to this further diversification of the cloth merchant-banker's interests that his determination to promote and build the Stockton & Darlington Railway — and hence the railways of the world — can be attributed.
G. Coates/Darlington Public Library

to attract investors during the war years and it was not until 1810 that Leonard Raisbeck, Recorder of Stockton, suggested a railway from the coalfield. This idea gained favour with the wealthy and influential Darlington cloth and linen merchant Edward Pease, who with other Darlington worthies produced the answer to the Auckland—Tees transport problem.

The answer was, of course, the Stockton & Darlington Railway (S&DR), the south Durham merchant magnates' long railway solution to the short ways of the North, whose evolution and grand opening in 1825 has been chronicled many times. Behind the opening festivities and celebrations of the S&DR in 1825, however, stood a considerable body of dissent. The celebrants were from Darlington, the dissenters from Stockton. For the Stockton contingent sought the shortest route, railway or canal, to the coalfields and saw no need for a long diversion through Darlington.

During the decade following Mr Raisbeck's suggestion rival rail and canal schemes were proposed and debated. In 1816 an idea for a canal throughout the 29½ miles from Teesmouth to Evenwood Colliery was the first suggestion by Christopher Tennant, an enterprising former sailor, now ship-owner, soon to become the driving force behind Stockton's determined efforts to provide a direct rail route between its port and the Auckland mines.

Tennant's canal proposal was approved at a meeting in Bishop Auckland in August 1818 but Edward Pease's influential backing for the railway and his assertion that such a scheme would give investors a return of at least 5% on capital invested won the day; the second Stockton & Darlington Railway Bill was given Royal Assent on 19 April 1821 and work started at Stockton in May 1822. There was, therefore, little love lost between the dignitaries of the two towns which had joined their names to form Teesside's first railway.

In September 1823, with the Stockton & Darlington already building, the Stockton party applied for recognition of the Tees & Weardale Railway (T&WR), planned to run from Willington, north of Bishop Auckland, to the Tees at Billingham Reach, some four miles east of Stockton. Willington was well to the north of the Auckland field, and the purpose of the T&WR was to serve the Coxhoe and

Quarrington collieries which were among the first to tap the huge reservoir of coal lying beneath the Durham magnesium limestone cap, which had been impenetrable before 1810. These collieries were leased from the Bishop of Durham by three unmarried ladies, daughters of the late General Hale. While no source describes the attributes of the Hale sisters, there is no doubt that their possession of the Coxhoe colliery lease made them highly desirable to the builders of the first Teesside railways. Thus the committee of the S&DR offered to buy the lease for these mines from the Misses Hale in 1821 at the time when the first bill was drawn up. Had an agreement been reached then, Joseph Pease, son of the venerable Edward, the prosperous S&DR Quaker founder member, said later, 'a branch of the Stockton & Darlington Railway would no doubt have been thrown out in the direction of Coxhoe'.

Subsequent T&WR applications by Christopher Tennant between 1823 and 1825 were defeated either through lack of capital or by the opposition of the S&DR committee, in league, in particular, with the Marquis of Londonderry through

It was Edward Pease's promise of '5% on capital invested' that won support for the first Teesside railway in 1818. It was a short step from the realisation of this promise to the first railway 'mania' in 1825. And here, surely, was not just the birth of railways but the real birth of capitalism. Investors were not so much interested in the new means of transport as in the profit they could make from it. Edward's son Joseph was the power behind the East Coast trunk railway route and saw this great project taken away by an even more powerful predator, George Hudson. Pease's financial manipulations were never found out, however, and Joseph Junior became Sir Joseph Whittwell Pease in 1882, Chairman of the Board of Directors of the NER in 1894, and was active in many charitable and philanthropic causes. His brother Arthur was particularly concerned with the 'spoiling industrial hand of my family'. Edward and his two sons, and Joseph's five sons, are shown in a late 19th century photo-montage.
G. Coates/Darlington Public Library

whose land the T&WR would run. Indeed, the Darlington contingent viewed every attempt to win a direct line as a breach of good faith in the 'agreement' which their defeat of 1818 had imposed upon their rivals.

But the T&WR supporters were determined to build their direct line and when the S&DR decided to cross the river to a new terminus at Middlesbrough in 1827, Christopher Tennant proposed another line from the coalfield, now to Haverton Hill, east of Stockton. Tennant named this new railway the Clarence Railway, after the Duke of Clarence, Lord High Admiral at the time and soon to be King William IV.

The Clarence Railway would run from a western terminus on the Deanery Estate, only a little north of the S&DR's Shildon depot, with an eastern branch into Stockton town itself. Also included in the Clarence's brief was a 'bough' thrown out northwards from the Clarence's 'trunk' line near Elstob, through Sedgefield to Ferryhill which stands in a natural gap in the great Durham limestone ridge. Branches from the 'bough' were to run westwards, to Chilton Colliery, south of Ferryhill, and to Byers Green from Ferryhill. Ferryhill would thus bring the Clarence Railway within striking

7

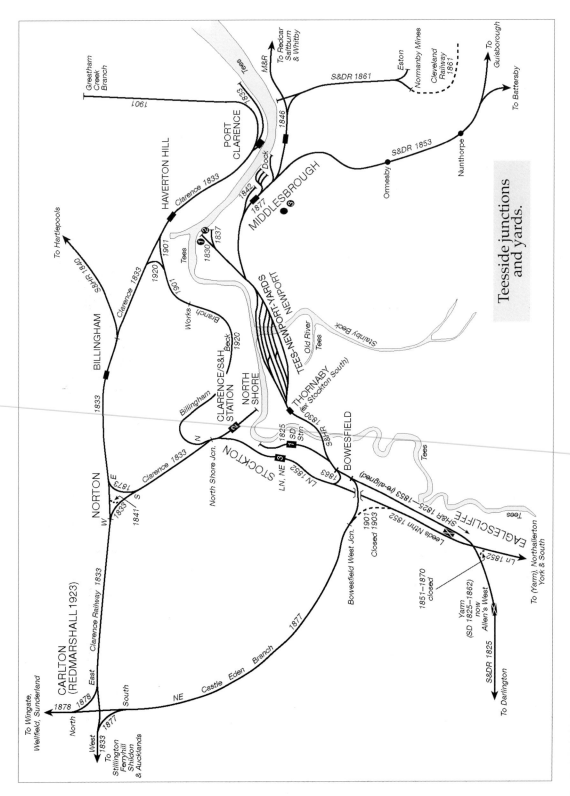

Teesside junctions and yards.

8

RAPID, SAFE, AND CHEAP TRAVELLING
By the Elegant *NEW RAILWAY COACH,*

THE UNION,

Which will COMMENCE RUNNING on the STOCKTON and DARLINGTON RAILWAY, on MONDAY
the 16th day of October, 1826,

And will call at Yarm, and pass within a mile of Middleton Spa, on its way from Stockton to Darlington, and *vice versa.*
FARES. Inside 1½d. — Outside, 1d. per Mile. Parcels in proportion.
No gratuities expected by the Guard or Coachman.

N. B. The Proprietors will not be accountable for any Parcel of more than £5. value, unless entered and paid for accordingly.
The UNION will run from the Black Lion Hotel and New Inn, Stockton, to the New Inn, Yarm, and to the Black Swan Inn, near the Croft Branch, Darlington ; at each of which Inns passengers and parcels are booked, and the times of starting may be ascertained, as also at the Union Inn, Yarm, and Talbot Inn, Darlington.
On the 19th and 20th of October, the Fair Days at Yarm, the Union will leave Darlington at six in the morning for Yarm, and will leave Yarm for Darlington again at six in the evening ; in the intermediate time, each day, it will ply constantly between Stockton and Yarm, leaving each place every half hour

distance of the Coxhoe and Quarrington collieries — whose lease, it was soon discovered, was now held by a founder member of the Clarence Railway!

This continued determination of its opponents caused the S&DR committee actually to declare 'War, therefore, open or concealed' upon the direct route upstarts. As W. W. Tomlinson pointed out, the second railway to be sanctioned 'in the north eastern portion of England was the outcome of competition rather than of emulation'. And, indeed, the fiercest competition would soon exist between these two pioneer railways, and with the opening of the huge Durham coalfield would escalate into war with new railways turning south from collieries on Wearside and Tyneside. The Teesside wars would become the 'War of the Three Rivers' as S&DR success and easier access to funds sparked off the first period of 'Railway Mania', a term which Professor Jack Simmons claimed was first used in 1825. Indeed, in that year of S&DR celebration, speculation in new industry was greatly encouraged by the culmination of a series of postwar economic

Above:
The first passenger 'train' — Stockton & Darlington Railway, 1826. Simply a rail-mounted stagecoach but fitted for each-way working so that the 'locomotive' could run round at journey's end. The service was due to start on 16 October; times and fares are given. *Ian Allan Library*

events, notably the abolition of the Bubble Act of 1720. This act restricted speculation after a wild 18th century scheme — or to use today's language, scam! — which actually gambled no less than the national debt in South Sea Islands speculation! The act's abolition in 1825 allowed promoters to press new projects on postwar industrial entrepreneurs just as they, free now of wartime market fears and fat on the proceeds of new industry and the brief postwar boom, looked round for profitable new investments.

During 1826, however, the Stockton & Darlington Railway was far from the prosperous concern which, together with the struggling Clarence, would settle the initial pattern for a railway system destined to serve the most important industrial area in the world's greatest

Right:
The first trains were composed of chaldron wagons, for the transport of both minerals and passengers! This example is shown at Faverdale Wagon Works, Darlington, in July 1925 during the centenary exhibition. It is the only survivor from the inaugural train. *Ian Allan Library*

Below:
In the midst of the first S&DR train was a dedicated passenger vehicle, a replica of which was marshalled in the 1925 centenary train. *Ian Allan Library*

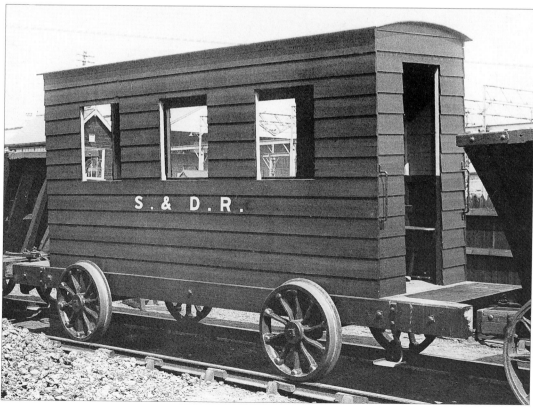

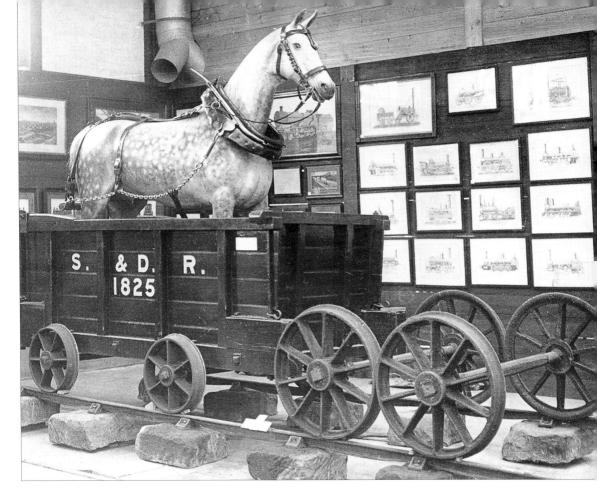

industrial economy. Still carrying a floating debt of £10,000 from the first construction of the line, on top of other considerable outstanding loans, and having been fined for incompletion of the pit branches west of Shildon — the very cause of the line — the S&DR was, in early 1826, unable to pay its current expenses. All this made the possibility of a direct rail route to the Tees a cause for real concern to the S&DR committee. It was saved, not for the only time, by advances from the huge personal fortune of founder member, Edward Pease. The situation then gradually improved with the apparent success of the railway attracting new and more readily available capital. The western branches, including the rich colliery-owning Reverend Luke Prattman's Haggerleases line, were open by 1830, together with the Croft branch to the Tees road crossing south of Darlington. With the opening of its extension from Stockton to Middlesbrough, therefore, the S&DR was in good order to offer battle to the puny competitor

Above:
An addition to horse-drawn coal trains in 1828 was a wagon attached to the end of the train in which the horse could ride on downhill runs. The word 'dandy' was applied at the time to anything 'posh' or showy and these soon won the name of 'dandy carts'. They were not introduced for humanitarian reasons, but a rested horse, or a well-maintained steam locomotive, both work better and last longer! The horses soon learned to board without prompting, and were quite willing to get down and work again when the run ended. Early S&DR rolling stock, *Locomotion* and the later *Derwent* are now displayed in the Darlington Railway Centre and Museum in the old North Road station in Darlington. *Ian Allan Library*

which still dared to threaten its monopoly of Tees traffic, even before starting to build.

Early in 1828 it was discovered that Mr Blanshard, who had tried to mediate with the S&DR committee in 1826, had paid an enormous amount for the Coxhoe Colliery lease in exchange for the support of the Misses Hale for the new railway. In May, to the chagrin of the merchants of Wear and Tyne, who saw their export trade challenged, Parliament approved both the S&DR Middlesbrough extension and, to the chagrin of Wear and Tyne *and* the Stockton & Darlington Railway, construction of the Clarence Railway.

Middlesbrough provided the S&DR with the answer to the acute navigation problems at Stockton, where the increasing volume of traffic was becoming unmanageable. In 1825, Middles-brough was an 'obscure and dreary village comprising little more than its name'. (J. Pease in the 1880s.) On 27 December 1830, however, Middlesbrough's single-figure population was increased by 600 when coal, rail and civic dignitaries, friends, families and hangers-on gathered there to celebrate the official opening of the new coal port. A passenger train hauled by a new locomotive, *Globe*, designed by Timothy Hackworth, who was now the first locomotive superintendent of the S&DR, conveyed many of the dignitaries from Darlington, bypassed Stockton at Bowesfield Junction (destined to become the busiest junction on Teesside), and crossed the new suspension bridge into Middlesbrough. The bridge was built in this style to conform with the demands of the Tees Navigation Co which envisaged considerable loss of earnings on shorter river journeys and became inevitably involved in the Teesside struggle for profit from the carriage of coals. A great celebration was held in the suitably furnished and decorated gallery beneath the new coal staithes which had, again, been designed by that retiring genius, Timothy Hackworth.

While the Clarence Railway actually started to build in 1830, it was unable to commence operations until 1833 when it found itself facing far more than the inevitable opening financial burdens — which included a loan of £100,000 from the Exchequer Loan Commissioners, a parliamentary body set up in 1817 to provide loans for large scale public works. The Deanery branch was successfully opposed and the new railway was obliged to take its Auckland coals from an end-on junction with the enemy at Simpasture, providing ready ammunition for the Darlington guns which immediately opened

fire: wagons leaving Shildon destined for the Clarence Railway were weighed individually at Thickley Weigh House while S&DR wagons were merely counted as they passed; Clarence coals were not allowed to be hauled at night, but, above, all the S&DR was able to cripple the Clarence by levying tolls of 2¼d per ton per mile over the 10 miles of S&DR rails which the Clarence had to use. This amounted to a surcharge of 2s 6d on every 53cwt chaldron wagon. The cost negated the advantage of the Clarence's shorter route which was legally obliged to open prematurely in August 1833 when the first loads of horse-drawn coal were hauled, in some places over stretches of temporary track, between Simpasture and Stockton.

At the eastern end of the Clarence's route, engineering works heavier than any encountered by the S&DR were needed to complete the main line: a succession of deep cuttings alternated with high embankments including that at Stillington reaching 75ft in height. One essential embankment on the crossing of Nunstainton Carrs, the continuation northwards of the once-navigable River Skerne's ancient flood plain from its confluence with the Tees at Croft, sank noisily and continually into the peat-bogs — the remains of which still flank today's East Coast main line — to the great

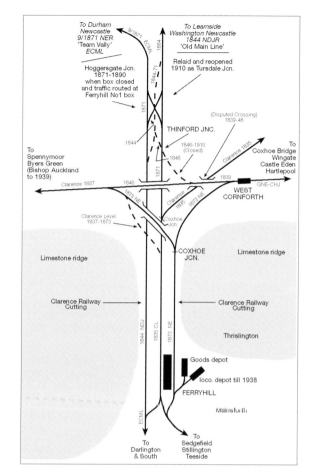

To Durham
Newcastle
9/1871 NER
'Team Vally'
ECML

To Leamside
Washington Newcastle
1844 NDJR
'Old Main Line'

9/1871 ECML

1844

Relaid and reopened
1910 as Tursdale Jcn.

Hoggersgate Jcn.
1871-1890
when box closed
and traffic routed at
Ferryhill No1 box

1844-71

1871

(Disputed Crossing)
1839-46

THINFORD JNC.

1844

1846-1910
(Closed)

1871

1846

Clarence 1835

To
Coxhoe Bridge
Wingate
Castle Eden
Hartlepool

To
Spennymoor
Byers Green
(Bishop Auckland
to 1939)

Clarence 1837

1846

1873 NE

Clarence 1835

1839

GNE-CHJ

1873 NE

WEST
CORNFORTH

Clarence Level
1837-1873

Coxhoe
Jcn

COXHOE
JCN.

Limestone ridge

Limestone ridge

Clarence Railway
Cutting

Clarence Railway
Cutting

1844 NDJ

1835 CL

1873 NE

Thrislington

Goods depot

loco. depot till 1938

FERRYHILL

ECML

Mainsforth

To
Darlington
& South

To
Sedgefield
Stillington
Teeside

satisfaction of the local villagers who heard their very own bog spirits sucking these demonic works down during the silence of the night!

But Clarence directors under Christopher Tennant had already shown how they were nothing if not determined, and now, with the lease for the Coxhoe and Quarrington mines in their pocket, they determined to tap this new source of revenue. Thus, by 1829 the original idea for a line to Ferryhill had blossomed into the City of Durham branch. Construction of this ambitious 'bough'

Left:
Ferryhill Gap: the Clarence Railway's way north.

Below:
Ferryhill in the 1930s with the locomotive depot to the right of the branch lines and station. In the right background the eastern limestone ridge looms over the Clarence Railway's great cutting. *Darlington*

Right:
The western cut of the ridge rises beyond what had become little more than the site of Ferryhill in 1968. The locomotive depot (closed in 1938 but retained) and goods depot, branches and sidings have almost disappeared.
The East Coast main line runs through.
Darlington

commenced from a junction with the main line just west of the great embankment at Stillington and ran northwards to the gap in the great limestone cap which sealed in the bulk of the Durham coal and which also effectively blocked the way north. Here, in 1835, the Clarence Railway, in debt, beset by irate landowners and obstructed at every move by the S&DR, blasted a cutting 67ft deep and 75yd wide at the top, from which was removed almost 100,000cu yd of limestone. This monumental excavation not only exposed 'an interesting section of the three lower divisions of the Permian system', as Tomlinson pointed out, but also opened the way north through Ferryhill into central Durham and its vast new coalfield. The Clarence's invaluable cutting also prepared the way for the northward extension in 1844 of the Great North of England Railway which, as the Newcastle & Darlington Junction Railway, would carry the east coast trunk route on from the Tees to the Wear and Tyneside, and Scotland.

The importance of the Ferryhill Gap has long been underestimated. On the west coast during the 1840s, gangs of railway navvies drove the rails up and over the hills of Cumberland and Westmorland in great inclined slopes which the steam engine has always been obliged to tackle at full tilt, the resulting everyday pyrotechnics ensuring the eternal fame of Shap and Beattock in the British railway world, while the fame of the Ferryhill Gap died with the last reverberations of the bankrupt Clarence Railway's final detonation. Yet this level route through the limestone, initially funnelling the heavy Durham mineral traffic southwards, and subsequently the busy East Coast passenger traffic north and south, was of considerably more economic importance than its West Coast counterpart.

The difficult Ferryhill line, its accompanying branches aimed at central Durham's new coal mines, the approaching national economic depression and bad luck effectively exhausted the Clarence Railway's resources. The Clarence's receipts for its first year stood at £2,206 6s 2d which barely paid the maintenance costs even before consideration of the £100,000 loan from the Exchequer Loan Commissioners! On 31 July 1834, this body took charge of the Clarence Railway and its subsequent management was directed from London.

In January 1834, the City of Durham branch reached the great cutting at Ferryhill, where it was terminated. A projected branch to Sherburn, a colliery village east of Durham City, took the Clarence beyond Ferryhill and as far as Coxhoe in 1835. Coxhoe became the terminus of both the Sherburn line and the Clarence Railway's northern endeavours, and the first coals were hauled from Ferryhill to Stockton North Shore on 16 January 1834.

In 1835, despite its financial difficulties, the

Clarence started to build the Chilton branch. The branch ran west from a point some two miles south of Ferryhill to Chilton Colliery. It was completed in May 1836 — seven months after the Chilton mine was closed because of 'unexpected difficulties'! Yet another source of Clarence revenue had come to nothing.

Meanwhile, the now prosperous S&DR laid double track throughout its system during 1831/2; it now owned 22 locomotives, mostly Hackworth six-wheelers, and in 1834 still further improved the flow of traffic by the use of locomotive haulage only on its lines. At last the worsening congestion caused by public haulage of rapidly increasing traffic by both horse and locomotive was done away with and the tremendous arguments, refusals to give way, accidents and actual fights between drivers and horse-leaders stopped — to a certain extent! For the Clarence coals were still obliged to be horse-drawn on S&DR rails and antagonism between company employees continued briskly west of Simpasture Junction.

In the east, things looked a little more optimistic for the Clarence. On 30 January 1834, the first coals were shipped from a single staithe at Haverton Hill, while, by 1835, three staithes were loading at a new, more easterly terminus

with the exotic name of Samphire Batts, no doubt noted for its 'batts' or beds of this salty sea salad. The name was soon changed to Port Clarence. By the end of 1835, however, the Clarence Railway's receipts had increased to but £3,189 11s 2d, less than a £1,000 gain on the preceding year, while coal tons hauled were 57,058 against 43,596 for 1834. The Exchequer Loan Commissioners were now owed some £150,000, even before running expenses were considered.

In 1831 Christopher Tennant had moved to Hartlepool on the north side of the Tees estuary. The harbour had been sadly neglected at the beginning of the 19th century, when it had long been a rubbish tip, but by 1831 reclamation had reopened the harbour to the sea, although the maximum spring tide depth was no more than 4ft. With coal mines now opening throughout the Durham field the indefatigable Tennant, certainly hardly profiting from his Clarence Railway, realised that Hartlepool provided a natural outlet for Durham coal and launched a joint project, both to open up the harbour for coal reception and to build a railway to serve it. At a meeting in Durham on 18 October 1831 George Stephenson, now recognised as a first-class railway engineer, was engaged to survey the route northwest.

The Hartlepool Dock & Railway Co (HD&R) opened in November 1835 with Christopher Tennant as Superintendent of Works. As sanctioned in 1832, the line was intended to run from Hartlepool to Moorsley Colliery, northeast of Durham City, with branches to serve other pits on the way. The line actually built ran only to Haswell Colliery; an uncertain economic climate, severe earthworks and a disinclination on the part of local coal owners to confirm their custom — the Durham & Sunderland Railway (D&SR) would soon provide a shorter route — curtailed the rest of the line. Colliery branches were built to Thornley and Quarrington Hill near the Clarence's Coxhoe terminus. Thornley coals were the first to be carried to Hartlepool on 1 January 1835. However, it was many months and several marine disasters later before the new docks were able to handle the coal traffic effectively.

As 1835 ended, therefore, Teesside gained a third railway which reached northwards into the new coalfield — only to be met by new lines running south from the Wear and the Tyne.

Above left:
The two-tender principle is portrayed by the magnificent *Derwent*, S&DR No 25 of 1845, which now rests with *Locomotion No 1* in the Darlington Museum.
N. E. Stead

Above:
No 23 *Wilberforce* of 1833 was one of 12 mineral engines built during 1832/3: the later six were 'Wilberforces', and the first six were 'Majestics'. They were designed by Hackworth as further improvements on *Royal George*. They had multiple-tubed boilers which further increased steaming efficiency, but were not without inevitable teething troubles. It was differences in tube numbers and arrangements which created two nominal classes, although, in those early days, it is correct to say that each and every engine carried 'detail differences'. The locomotives were built by Hackworth's own works at Shildon (six), Robert Stephenson & Co (three) and R. & W. Hawthorn (three) — mass-production and contracting out had arrived!
Locomotive Publishing Co/Ian Allan Library

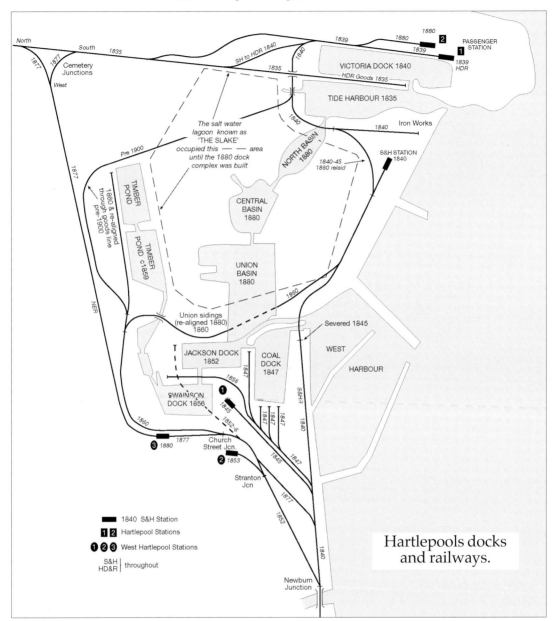

North

South   1835

1877   1877

Cemetery
Junctions

West

1839   1880   1880

2   PASSENGER
STATION

SH to HDR 1840   1839   1839   1

1840   1839
HDR

1835   VICTORIA DOCK 1840   1880

HDR Goods 1835

TIDE HARBOUR 1835

1840   Iron Works

1840

The salt water
lagoon known as
'THE SLAKE'
occupied this —— —— area
until the 1880 dock
complex was built

Pre 1900

S&H STATION
1840

NORTH BASIN
1880

1840-45
1860 relaid

1877

TIMBER
POND

1860 & re-aligned
through goods line
pre-1900

CENTRAL
BASIN
1880

TIMBER
POND c1859

UNION
BASIN
1880

NER

1860

Union sidings
(re-aligned 1880)
1860

Severed 1845

WEST

JACKSON DOCK
1852

COAL
DOCK
1847

HARBOUR

1847

SWAINSON
DOCK 1856

1   1845

1852-6

1847
1847
1847
1840

S&H R

1860

3   1880   1877

Church
Street Jcn.

2   1853

1845
1847

Stranton
Jcn

1877

1852

1840   S&H Station
1   2   Hartlepool Stations
1   2   3   West Hartlepool Stations
S&H
HD&R   throughout

Hartlepools docks
and railways.

1840

Newburn
Junction

When the HD&R's final assent was passed by
Parliament in June 1834 it was accompanied by
acts for the Durham Junction Railway and the
Durham & Sunderland Railway, both of which
intended to reach Haswell from the north. The
first was a branch of the 38-mile cross-country
Stanhope & Tyne Railway; the branch was not
opened until 1838 and ran no further than
Rainton, to become in 1844, a small but vital
component in the new north-south trunk route.

The D&SR, however, opened in July 1836, only
eight months after the HD&R, and actually
reached Haswell, only 9½ miles from
Sunderland compared with 14 from Hartlepool.
The stubborn determination of the HD&R,
however, prevented through running between
Hartlepool and Sunderland until North Eastern
Railway (NER) days. The 'War of the Three
Rivers' was now declared.

Right:
A less dignified end came to No 20 *Adelaide*, the last of the 'Wilberforces'. After withdrawal in 1848 she spent her last days immobilised, but still, as her front end shows here, working hard, grinding clay in a factory yard in Saltburn at the eastern end of the (S&D) line! This picture also shows the firing method 'within' the smokebox. *R. E. Bleasdale/Locomotive Publishing Co/Ian Allan Library*

Below:
'J27' 0-6-0T No 65868 and brake come tender-first from Hartlepool past Newburn Junction by the sea in September 1956, 125 years after Christopher Tennant moved to Hartlepool and began to open up its dock for coal from Durham. *G. M. Staddon/N. Stead collection*

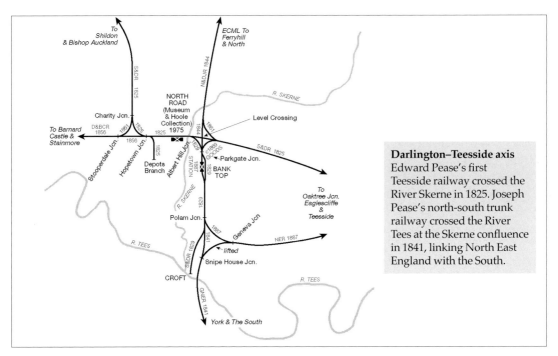

Darlington–Teesside axis
Edward Pease's first Teesside railway crossed the River Skerne in 1825. Joseph Pease's north-south trunk railway crossed the River Tees at the Skerne confluence in 1841, linking North East England with the South.

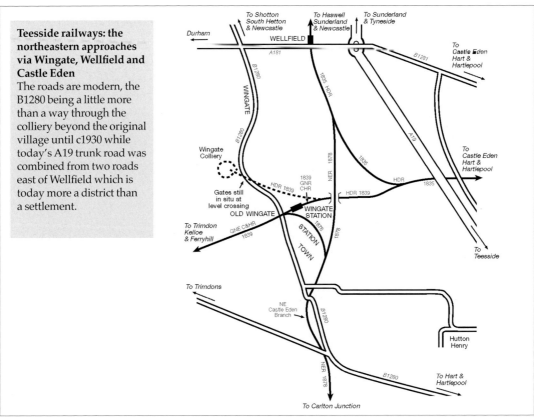

Teesside railways: the northeastern approaches via Wingate, Wellfield and Castle Eden
The roads are modern, the B1280 being a little more than a way through the colliery beyond the original village until c1930 while today's A19 trunk road was combined from two roads east of Wellfield which is today more a district than a settlement.

2. Many Railways

On 24 December 1835, Joseph Pease and Christopher Tennant confronted each other at a public meeting in Stockton. Pease foresaw a trunk railway, the Great North of England Railway (GNER), which would link Northumberland and Durham to York, where it would in turn join up with the proposed York & North Midland Railway, thence head southwards again, with the London & Birmingham Railway to that inevitable capital goal, London. This north-to-south trunk line would also, of course, considerably increase S&DR revenue.

Tennant complained bitterly about the GNER's projected route through Darlington which would again bypass Stockton, while Pease was concerned about the 'sinister' proposals of the Clarence Railway. The old antagonisms lived on. The 'sinister' proposals were for two lines which would effectively extend Clarence branches. The Durham & South West Junction Railway (D&SWJR) was Tennant's own attempt to gain the Clarence's original goal by linking the Auckland coalfield to the Clarence's unfortunate Chilton branch, while the South Durham Railway planned to run from the lead mining district around Wolsingham, through the west Durham collieries, and then to join the Clarence's Byers Green branch. Both lines would then run through to Tennant's new HD&R.

In 1836, these Teesside extension proposals were stopped by local landowners, although both were well thought of by more long-sighted railway proposers, including George Hudson, who saw the lines as useful links into his own expanding railway system. In the event, the two rejected Teesside lines were almost immediately reconstituted under new names late in 1836, although the D&SWJR's renewed attempt to connect Auckland to the Tees finally died in 1837. The SDR reappeared as two separate entities: the *new* SDR — renamed from the Weardale Railway — assisted in the completion of the Clarence's delayed Byers Green branch and, ultimately, was opened between Willington and Byers Green on 12 June 1840 — as the West Durham Railway! On that day coals and the Mayor of Stockton were carried from Willington to Stockton behind Clarence Railway Hackworth six-wheelers.

Meanwhile, Tennant's attention was diverted from Auckland to the eastern end of the Clarence where the eastern phoenix of the *original* South Durham Railway, under the grandiose title of the Great North of England, Clarence & Hartlepool Junction Railway (GNE,C&HJR), sanctioned in 1837, threatened both HD&R and Clarence traffic. It proposed to run independently from the projected Wingate Colliery branch of the HD&R through to a junction with the Byers Green branch at Ferryhill where it would also join the proposed new GNER trunk route. If given the chance, it would tap the long-suffering Clarence's finally, if jointly, won access to the Auckland coalfield. It will soon be seen, however, that the Clarence was able to block the GNE, C&HJR's proposed junction at Ferryhill for almost a decade and need never have feared its competition.

The complications of 1835/6 on Teesside were but a faint echo of the nationwide scramble to build railways which swept the country in these years. The 20 years and more of experiment with railways and steam locomotion in the North, notably the unexpected success of passenger traffic, realised belatedly by the S&DR, and proved by the Liverpool & Manchester Railway since 1829, were closely watched by prospective investors until, in 1835, everybody suddenly wanted a railway. Parliament was presented with some 57 proposals during 1836/7, the second or 'little mania' as Professor Eric Hobsbawm has termed it. However, by 1837 this 'little mania' ended abruptly as bad harvests and a downturn in trade plunged Britain's economic boom into recession. In the new industrial towns unemployment hit thousands who were already surviving on subsistence wages. The 'labouring poor' suffered untold misery in unthinkable conditions.

Hobsbawm points out that 'at no other period in modern British history have the common people been so persistently, profoundly and often desperately dissatisfied'.

Many newly projected railway lines, such as the impoverished Clarence Railway's extensions, were curtailed or cancelled at this crucial time for Britain's new industrial society, but construction generally continued, driven on by the great armies of relatively well-paid navvies, precursors of the new railway 'labouring elite'.

During the 'little mania' years, 44 new railway companies were authorised nationwide, but only three were sanctioned in the North East where

Below:
By the 1840s, passengers travelled in purpose-built rail stagecoaches. Luggage was still carried on the roof as is prettily pointed out on this S&DR composite now at the North Road station museum in Darlington. *Ian Allan Library*

pioneering 'first mania' lines had already drawn the basic pattern for the developing railway system. Two were granted on Tyneside, while Joseph Pease's north-south GNER was sanctioned between York and Gateshead. Pease would soon lose this valuable trunk line to that unscrupulous 'railway king', George Hudson, as he pushed his kingdom northwards. Erstwhile draper, Mayor of York, MP and now thriving railway entrepreneur, in 1835/6 Hudson's main concern was to link York with London and he was involved in several rival trunk schemes which had emerged from the 1830s mania. As this great rail route battle pressed northwards, ambitious eyes inevitably turned towards Pease's GNER project, set to cut directly through the Three Rivers battlefield, and it was not long before Hudson determined to add this major earldom to his expanding kingdom and also to make the North East into a considerable 'royal fief'.

By March 1839, the HD&R branch was

Above:
The GNE,C&HJR used the HD&JR's Wingate Colliery branch to start its westward course in 1839 and when the Castle Eden branch crossed and connected with it in 1878, the 'Castle Eden–Hart northeast corner crossroads' complex was completed to complement Carlton and Norton at the southeast Teesside gateway 'corner crossroads'. The remains of Wingate station are seen here left of the box, the 1878 spur to the Castle Eden line on the right after leaving the main line through the station just after the bridge over the B1280 behind the photographer. Beyond the station the colliery branch went off left to cross the B1280 on the level. Today, the still-intact crossing gates faithfully protect the old colliery site from North Eastern ghosts. *Darlington*

completed to Wingate and in July the predatory GNE,C&HJR approached the Clarence at Ferryhill after some fearsome engineering feats westward from Wingate, round the eastern ridge of the limestone cap. (Wingate station was actually situated in Station Town, immediately south of Wingate colliery village.) At Ferryhill the GNE,C&HJR prepared to make its proposed junctions with the north-south GNE trunk line and the Clarence. On approaching Ferryhill, however, it was discovered that while powers had been obtained to cross and link with the GNER, no permission had been obtained to cross or join the Clarence Railway. This simple omission played right into the Clarence's hands and it was able to hold up completion of the connection, which would have diverted its traffic directly into Hartlepool, for no less than seven years. By this time, in 1845, the HD&R leased the GNE,C&HJR, just one year before both companies were leased by the newly formed York & Newcastle Railway. The link between Hartlepool and the West Auckland coalfields was finally established and coal travelled from the west Durham fields through to both north and south Teesside ports.

Meanwhile, on 9 February 1841 Christopher Tennant's Stockton & Hartlepool Railway (S&HR) opened. The S&HR was a wayleave linkline connecting the Clarence's Stockton branch to its main line via a curve laid in south to east at Norton, then leaving the Clarence just east of Billingham to run through Greatham to Hartlepool. Over the next 35 years Norton Junction, together with Bowesfield and then Carlton, grew to form together the intensely busy western gateway into Teesside; but Tennant's initial intention, to counter the GNE,C&HJR's Hartlepool access, was negated by that line's long controversy with the Clarence at Ferryhill. Christopher Tennant, however, at first champion of the Clarence 'direct route', then of Hartlepool's renaissance, would never know this. He died suddenly while on a promotional visit to Leeds in 1839. As a result of this trip Tennant's last achievement was to inaugurate the through carriage of fish by rail.

Left:
North of Norton and Billingham and going well towards Greatham, T. Worsdell 'A' (LNER 'F8') class 2-4-2T No 1582 shows her paces on the S&HR/LNR main line with a Class A train.
H. Gordon Tidey

Below:
One hundred and twenty years after Christopher Tennant's final fatal railway negotiation for Hartlepool had initiated the carriage of fish by rail, 'J72' No 68683 rests between marshalling moves in Hartlepool fish dock in August 1959.
*G. M. Staddon/
N. Stead collection*

A daily service started in 1841 from Hartlepool into Yorkshire and Lancashire. He had, however, seen the first-fruits of his Hartlepool dock and rail project multiply threefold between 1836 and 1840, while in the latter year Hartlepool received the first cargoes of a fast-developing timber import trade from Baltic and Canadian ports. Tennant did not die unsung and a long and romantic poem to the 'Great Sire of Railways! Father of the Clarence!' is preserved in Darlington library.

In spite of the deepening recession of the 1840s, railway construction continued. The West Coast trunk line was driven over the Cumbrian fells during the 1840s and, as a Parliamentary Commission set up to report upon rail communication between England and Scotland favoured this route, it became imperative that the East Coast interests complete Pease's GNER. The easy southern section opened between Darlington and York on 4 January 1841, crossing the Tees just south of Darlington on a new bridge at Croft, using its entire authorised capital in the process.

A year later, the GNER went on under new management and a new name. For George Hudson, with his many holdings south of York, was able to provide the extra capital needed to purchase the rights to the northern section of the struggling new company and then to take the East Coast trunk line forward as the Newcastle & Darlington Junction Railway (N&DJR) — utilising the Clarence Railway's great Ferryhill cutting to head on across the Wear to the Tyne, amalgamating and connecting five independent lines on the way. Once established in the north, Hudson determined finally to destroy the Pease influence and even had designs on Teesside's ports.

While Hudson's N&DJR drove north from Darlington to Gateshead during 1842-4 a new dock was opened at Middlesbrough in May 1842 with accommodation for 150 ships, served by a branch from the S&DR which included 10 new coal drops and 10 double sidings with standing room for 1,200 wagons. The S&DR advanced most of the £120,000 cost of this ambitious slump-time project. In January 1842 Shildon Tunnel was opened after almost three years of delving through the western skirts of the limestone ridge. Having 'cut the corner', the S&DR entered Bishop Auckland in 1843 to meet the Bishop Auckland & Weardale Railway which had just arrived from Crook and Weardale where the Derwent Iron Co struggled to keep the western end of the ambitious old Stanhope & Tyne Railway of 1834 solvent.

Below:
The 'Wild West' line from Stainmore entered Bishop Auckland — from the *east*, after first joining the 1842 line from Shildon. Stainmore trains used the inside of the 1856 north to east curve, and here a 'Wild West' train awaits departure opposite old 'G5' 0-4-4T No 67342 standing on the 'outside', blower on, ready to go home on the 4.15pm to Durham and Sunderland on 23 July 1957. *I. S. Carr*

The S&DR would soon help out these struggling lines in this new western outpost — to its cost.

In 1842, the Clarence was in such financial straits that the shareholders had to find £80,000 to keep the company running. Similarly, the West Durham Railway which now brought coal to the Clarence at Byers Green actually closed down completely for several weeks until it too was bailed out by its shareholders. In the same lean year the thriving S&DR was able to pay its shareholders 15%, whereas the average dividend over 36 railway companies nationwide was 5.75%.

The great recession culminated in a general strike in 1842 after which the economy began to pick up and, with trade unions no longer illegal, there began a slow realisation by both managers and workers that they belonged, unavoidably, to the same working family and must tackle their differences as 'Industrial Relations'. In 1843, capital again became more freely available and the more shrewd financial observers foresaw the approach of the third, or, for Hobsbawm,

'gigantic mania' as applications for new lines poured in. Indeed, by January 1846, no fewer than 815 railway schemes had been presented to Parliament nationwide. The Commons set up a special Committee on the Classification of Railway Bills and three junior ministers, including one W. E. Gladstone, attempted to organise a national system of independent railways — and were pointedly ignored.

The national recovery was owed in no small measure to this fast developing new railway which brought employment and prosperity to the land just when it was needed. Professor Hobsbawm notes that: 'Such a vast economic stimulus, coming at the very moment when the economy was passing through its most catastrophic slump of the century, could hardly have been better timed.'

Just as mining 'invented and developed the *railway*' in the North East, Hobsbawm also stated that 'The railways were largely responsible for the doubling of British iron output between the middle 1830s and the middle 1840s.' In the 1780s, iron production did not exceed 100,000 tons per annum, but this figure leapt to 1 million tons by 1835, which in turn doubled by 1847. Innovations in technology, notably smelting with coke, meant that coke ovens and iron foundries were now located close to the coalfields on which they depended. Most of this new production occurred on Teesside; thus, in 1841, Middlesbrough Ironworks was opened — on land purchased from Joseph Pease!

While the rest of the country steadily inflated the great 'manic' bubble and railway systems were mooted to serve virtually every hamlet in Britain, the railways of Teesside carried steadily on with the consolidation and operation of the increasingly busy routes which had sprung from their own very first mania some 20 years earlier. The beleaguered Clarence Railway, however, was unable to benefit from the new prosperity and in 1844 the S&HR took out a 21-year lease on its sister 'Tennant railway'. Two years later, George Hudson's failure to purchase the Clarence was his only setback in a 'royal progress' during which he virtually took charge of railway and dock installations throughout the North East. In 1845, in what he admitted as 'the hardest bargain he ever drove', Hudson offered extremely generous terms in order to snatch the GNER from the clutches of the Great Northern

Railway (GNR), another predator advancing directly from the south in direct defiance of Hudson's Midland route. One year later, Hudson was able to amalgamate the GNER and N&DJR into the York & Newcastle Railway, bringing the HD&R and GNE,C&HJR into his fold in the process, while further amalgamation north of Newcastle in 1847 formed the York, Newcastle & Berwick Railway. Hudson now controlled the East Coast main line between York and Berwick — although the line terminated at Gateshead until the completion of the High Level Bridge in August 1849.

During these years of 'manic' railway construction throughout the country and consolidation of the first railways in the North East, the nation enjoyed a continued general increase in prosperity. As J. F. C. Harrison has pointed out, 'By 1847, Britain just had more of everything: more raw cotton imported, more tons of coal dug out, more miles of railways built — also more crime — than ever before.'

Amid this blooming prosperity Teesside's first two railways, the Stockton & Darlington and its eternal rival the (leased) Clarence, still stood solidly independent across George Hudson's great amalgamation, the York, Newcastle & Berwick (YN&BR). In 1849, however, Hudson was found guilty of financial malpractice and his kingdom crashed about him, while, with a veritable sea of railways proposing to flood the nation, and having weathered the 'Hungry Forties' better than any other railway afloat, that pioneering flagship of public railways, the affluent Stockton & Darlington, struck a rock. In 1846, the S&DR had leased the new Middlesbrough & Redcar Railway, together with an interest in impecunious West Auckland lines which the over-confident committee envisaged would eventually carry their good fortune clear across to Carlisle, all at a promised rental of 6% on the share capital!

In the event, the Wear Valley Railway was never financially able to leave the vale after which it was named and the S&DR was saddled with debts which exceeded its curtailed revenue. It was perhaps this disastrous speculation which brought about the alleged talks between Joseph Pease and the Hartlepool directors apropos the previously unthinkable carriage of S&DR coals to Hartlepool — and even amalgamation — in early 1850. Ralph Ward Jackson, a Hartlepool

solicitor, stepped in while Pease, uncharacter-
istically but quite understandably, hesitated, and
by 1851 Ward Jackson had secured a perpetual
extension of the 1842 lease on the Clarence
Railway for the S&HR. This doughty successor
to Christopher Tennant then amalgamated the
S&HR with the Hartlepool West Harbour & Dock
Co to create the West Hartlepool Harbour &
Railway Co (WHH&R) — and the new town of
West Hartlepool. The WHH&R was incorporated
in May 1853 after further enlargement of the docks
which had developed from Tennant's original
salvation in 1835. Ward Jackson continued
Tennant's promotion of the Hartlepools' success
and is indeed better remembered as a founding
father than his worthy predecessor, perhaps
because of his eventual emulation of George
Hudson in his over-zealous interpretation
of the law in the protection of the railway's

assets which finally led to scandal and his
unfortunate disgrace — always more
newsworthy than straight dealing.

A remarkable discovery in 1850, however, not
only miraculously refloated the S&DR but also
guaranteed the future prosperity of Teesside
and all its railways — and also rekindled
hostilities between the pioneer Teesside railway
neighbours which would result in a last decade
of aggressive Teesside railway expansion.

From their Wearside ironworks situated on the
Auckland coalfield since 1846, Messrs Bolckow
& Vaughan sent engineers in search of iron ore
and in 1850 they found a rich seam starting at
Eston, some 10 miles southeast of Middlesbrough and hardly three miles from the S&DR's
new lessee, the Middlesbrough & Redcar
Railway (M&RR) — currently contributing to
the S&DR's financial tribulations! The S&DR's
parlous position was reversed when Bolckow &
Vaughan constructed a branch line to the M&RR;
this was soon followed by a second further east
when the Derwent Iron Co opened its own mine
at Upleatham. The Derwent company's works
were at Consett — the end of the S&DR's leased
Weardale liabilities and the western terminus of
the S&DR system. Far from being the end of the
line, however, this 54-mile trip alone would soon
earn the S&DR £10,000 per annum. The lucky
S&DR ship was afloat again and its shares
recovered; dividends, having dropped from

13% to 4%, now jumped straight back to 10%.

Between 1852 and 1854, the S&DR dropped its own branch down to Guisborough from Middlesbrough in order to reach mines which were rapidly opening along the newly discovered seam. But nothing is perfect, and a drawback to the vast quantity of newly discovered Yorkshire iron ore was its low quality. In order for good-quality iron to be forged, a mix with higher-quality haematite ore was necessary. Such ore had long been mined in Cumberland and supplied to the early North Eastern iron foundries (hence Bolckow & Vaughan's initial siting) via the Newcastle & Carlisle Railway. With the North Yorks 'Klondyke' ore discovery and the resulting rash of ironworks on Teesside, the need for the distant haematite ore became as vital as that for the readily available coal and low-grade Yorkshire ore — and the high-grade ore lay directly west of Auckland; the only barrier was the Pennine Range!

The first step across England's 'backbone' was taken in 1852 when a group, which included several S&DR committee members, proposed a railway from Darlington to Barnard Castle, upon which the recently formed WHH&R flexed new muscles and proposed its own approach to the west from Bishop Auckland. Once again war was to be waged between Teesside antagonists. The Hartlepool plan had considerable backing; the YN&BR, together with the Wearside and Tyneside towns which it served, preferred the more convenient northern approach — and an end to the autocracy of a revitalised Joseph Pease! However, this round finally went to the S&DR committee which opened the Darlington & Barnard Castle Railway amid great rejoicing on 8 July 1856.

Another innovation by the S&DR in 1856 was the construction of the Shildon Tunnel branch which left the Bishop Auckland line just north of the 1842 tunnel and looped round to West Auckland and the Haggerleases branch, thus rendering the rope-hauled Brusselton inclines redundant and considerably speeding traffic.

In 1861, the Pennines were finally crossed by the formidable gradients and monumental viaducts which lifted the South Durham & Lancashire Union Railway (SD&LUR) — again worked by the S&DR — over Stainmore, down into Kirkby Stephen, then on to junctions with London & North Western Railway (LNWR) satellites at Tebay and Penrith, the latter reached in 1862 via a branch of the Eden Valley Railway. At the eastern end in 1863, the S&DR shamelessly constructed the Hartlepool's proposed route from Bishop Auckland to Barnard Castle via a loop to the convenient new 'Tunnel branch'. Heavy two-way traffic commenced immediately — haematite ore between Cumberland and Durham, and coke from Durham to Cumberland — and this

Right:
Beyond Billingham the Clarence went on to its termini at Haverton Hill and then Port Clarence where Bell Bros built their ironworks in 1853.
K. Taylor/Darlington

continued for just a century until the Stainmore line's untimely closure in January 1962.

Meanwhile, the newly constituted WHH&R prepared its new deep dock, the Jackson Dock at West Hartlepool, for the transport of still more coal from the developing Durham coalfield while, in 1852, it gained access to the South when the Leeds Northern finally reached Teesside at Stockton — its goal since authorisation in 1845. The WHH&R next looked greedily across the Tees at the riches which the S&DR was reaping from transport of the newly discovered iron ore deposits and in 1857, ever-determined, the 'implacable enemies', as C. J. Allen described the WHH&R, having lost the bid for the western haematite ore traffic to the S&DR, declared war on the eastern front by proposing a ferry to cross the Tees from Port Clarence (where Bell Bros' Ironworks had been built in 1853 to be near the coal) to Cargo Fleet. From there, a new railway would run down to Guisborough and the ironstone mines beyond, crossing the S&DR's satellite lines on the way. This, of course, prompted violent objections from the S&DR and, just to make it even more traditional, the Tees Conservancy Commissioners objected to any further crossings of the river. The old rivalries flared anew and led to a tremendous parliamentary battle in 1858 which culminated in Autumn 1860 with actual riverside fighting between the rival parties. This latest battle, almost 50 years

after the Darlington committee declared, 'War, therefore, open or concealed', has actually earned the historic title Battle of the Tees. The final outcome in 1860 was a resounding win for the Hartlepool party which was given all it asked for. A consolation for the S&DR in 1858 was authorisation to amalgamate with all its leased lines and also to extend its eastern terminus from Redcar to Saltburn, thus improving access to the Upleatham and Skelton ore mines.

The entry of the Leeds Northern Railway (LNR) into Teesside from its YN&BR crossing at Northallerton in 1852, opened an alternative (if much slower) route, south to north, in conjunction with the Hartlepool and D&S railways. Consequently, a last burst of Darlington v Stockton & Hartlepool competition flared; for, as the battles for the mineral traffic were fought east and west, so the LNR and the YN&BR embarked on a no-win rates war for passenger traffic north and south. Each company alternated in cheaper fares until the impossible spiral finally ended in 1854 with amalgamation between the LNR, the YN&BR and the York & North Midland, the latter 'Hudson railway' continuing the trunk line south until joint running over the direct Great Northern Railway to Doncaster was agreed in 1864. The YN&BR was the senior partner in this initial agreement and vested the other two companies into a new company — the North Eastern Railway.

Above:
The interior remains of Saltburn's typically S&DR one-platform station look damp, empty and roofless in this February 1970 view. *Ian Allan Library*

Below:
The outside of Saltburn station is also deserted except for the inevitable motor cars in 1973. *Ian Allan Library*

Above:
George Stephenson's *Locomotion*, Stockton & Darlington Railway No 1, was billed as 'a superior Loco Motive Travelling Engine, of the most improved construction', by the committee of the S&DR in their press announcement of the opening of the new railway. *Locomotion* was a development of *Blucher*, Stephenson's first steam locomotive, which used a cog-wheel transmission, a system he had 'poached' from the earlier Wylam and Kenton engines. *Locomotion* was the first of a class of four, *Hope, Black Diamond* and *Diligence* being the sister engines. They were not really successful despite the account of the grand opening. Their worst fault was shortage of steam, a problem which was admirably solved in 1827 by Timothy Hackworth. *Locomotive Publishing Co/Ian Allan Library*

Royal George, S&DR No 5, which began to haul coal trains regularly and most successfully in November 1827. Designed by Timothy Hackworth, recently appointed S&DR locomotive manager, and assembled under his supervision at the S&DR Shildon Works, No 5 carried a boiler almost 13ft long (No 1's was 10ft) which had been discarded from an experimental locomotive. Six wheels were needed to carry this big boiler which contained a U-shaped flue tube. This meant that the chimney exhausted, being at the same end as the fire. The cylinders were now mounted outside the boiler and drove vertical connecting rods coupled directly to the crank pins of the rear coupled wheels. The doubled heating surface and a coned blastpipe in the chimney improved locomotive 'breathing' considerably and there is no doubt that *Royal George* secured the future of the steam locomotive at a time when the unreliable

performance of its Stephenson predecessors meant the survival of steam traction was far from certain. *Locomotive Publishing Co/Ian Allan Library*

The Rainhill Trials of 1829 were called by the directors of the Liverpool & Manchester Railway to prove the superiority of the locomotive over the stationary engine, and then to decide the best locomotive for the new line. The winner of the contest, *Rocket*, now shares with *Flying Scotsman* the claim of being the most famous steam locomotive in the world, and a number of full-size replicas have been built. *Real Photos*

Below:
Rocket defeated Hackworth's Shildon-built *Sans Pareil* thanks to a faulty cylinder supplied by Stephenson! While neither worked on Teesside, each became the precursor of a well-established main line passenger type. *Sans Pareil*, worked successfully for many years on the Bolton & Leigh Railway. The replica, seen here, is kept at Shildon's Hackworth Museum and steams during the summer. *Ian Allan Library*

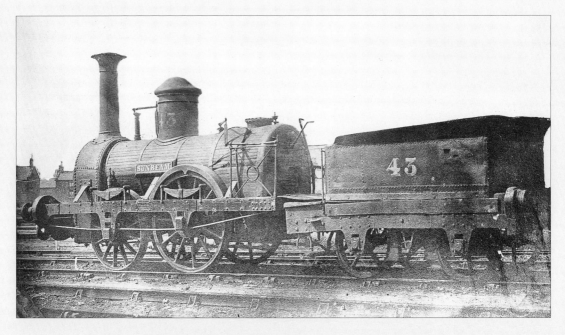

PASSENGER LOCOMOTIVE DEVELOPMENTS

Above:
While *Rocket* was the prototype of a class of L&MR 0-2-2s, subsequent single-driver development can be seen in the S&DR's inside-cylinder 2-2-0 No 28 *Sunbeam* (later No 43) built in 1837 by Hawthorn's.
Locomotive Publishing Co/Ian Allan Library

Below:
S&DR No 41 *Dart* of 1840, by Hackworth, continued his four-coupled development, again with inside cylinders. The multiple buffers were necessary for working either chaldrons or 'modern' stock.
Locomotive Publishing Co/Ian Allan Library

SIX-COUPLED LOCOMOTIVES

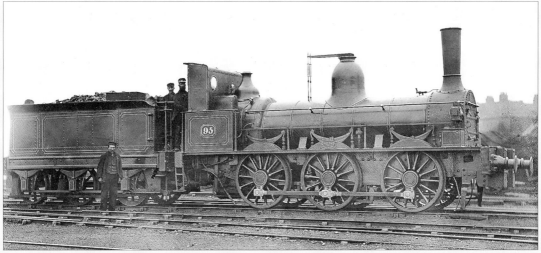

Top:
From 1840, Hackworth concentrated on his own Shildon engineering works where he continued to manufacture locomotives. His dual-tendered 0-6-0s worked most of the mineral trains on Teesside's railways while his successor on the S&DR, William Bouch, took up the Stephenson long-boilered idea and produced No 35 *Commerce* in 1847. The connecting rods, uniquely, worked closely *inside* the coupling rods and were constructed in a curious circular section in order to accommodate the leading crank pins. *Commerce* was surely the prototype for many thousands of plain old six-wheelers which have faithfully plodded through many millions of revenue-earning but unremarked miles along the railways of the world. *Locomotive Publishing Co/Ian Allan Library*

Above:
From *Commerce* grew an ever-larger fleet of strong but simple 0-6-0 freight engines. They were built by many different contractors with many inevitable individualities. NER Classes 13, 93 and 1001 all tried in vain to standardise these early types, while attempts are still made today to identify them individually. The first S&DR engines were all named, like No 95 *Elephant*, built in 1855 by Gilkes Wilson, and seen here unnamed after the 1863 amalgamation, but still nicely lined out in green. Other names, such as *Swallow* and *Lily*, were not so appropriate for bluff old goods engines. *Locomotive Publishing Co/ Ian Allan Library*

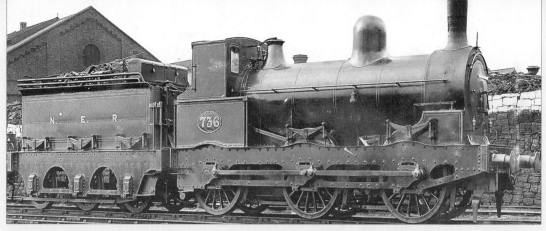

Above:
Many of these 0-6-0s had outside frames, including No 736 of Fletcher's '708' class, seen here as rebuilt by the unfortunate Alexander McDonnell whose serious attempts at standardisation after Fletcher's *laissez-faire* approach were not appreciated by the loco men.
Locomotive Publishing Co/Ian Allan Library

Above:
Some of the early 0-6-0s were rebuilt, such as Stephenson-built No 1177 *Osborne* of 1865.
Locomotive Publishing Co/Ian Allan Library

Below:
Seen in later years, No 1177 has become a 'new-age' Worsdell engine in all but wheels and cab.
Locomotive Publishing Co/Ian Allan Library

Above:
At first, locomotives marshalled their own trains, but as the number and length of trains increased, engines with integral water tanks and coal bunkers rather than separate tenders were introduced to do the yard jobs. The tank engine became an essential part of the short-range railway scene and, by the 1860s, tank engines worked as pilots in marshalling yards throughout the system. No 1369 was an 1870s example of a Fletcher 'stove-pipe era' shunting engine. *Locomotive Publishing Co/Ian Allan Library*

Below:
No 73 was a 2-4-0 well tank of about the same era and was used on local passenger trains. *Locomotive Publishing Co/Ian Allan Library*

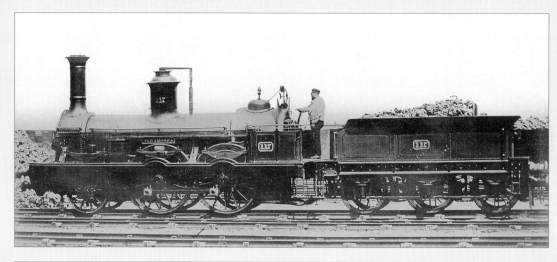

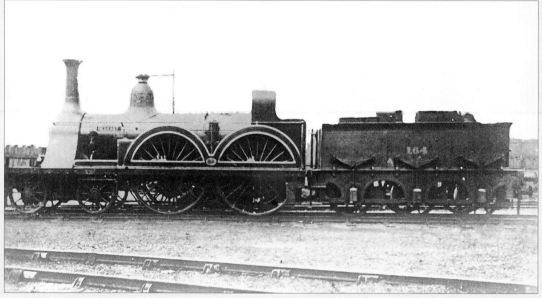

Top:
The 'Woodlands' class locomotives were built between 1848 and 1860 for the S&DR by Alfred Kitching of Hope Town Foundry, Darlington. A powerful 2-4-0, whose close-coupled wheels and long boiler show Stephenson affinities, No 117 *Nunthorpe* is in original condition.
Locomotive Publishing Co/Ian Allan Library

Above:
Brougham and *Lowther*, Nos 160 and 161, were built to Bouch's unconventional specification in 1860 for the initial opening of the Stainmore line to Brough. They were the first *true* bogie engines; Daniel Gooch's GWR engines of 1855 were really 2-2-4-0s. The unusually humane cabs against the Pennine winters were not appreciated by the crews; footplatemen were already a singular breed! In 1862, the 'Brougham' pair were followed by four more bogie engines, the 'Saltburns', with coupled wheels no less than 7ft in diameter. No 164 *Belfast* is shown in original condition with 'naked' splashers and simple weatherboard — as requested by the men!
Locomotive Publishing Co/Ian Allan Library

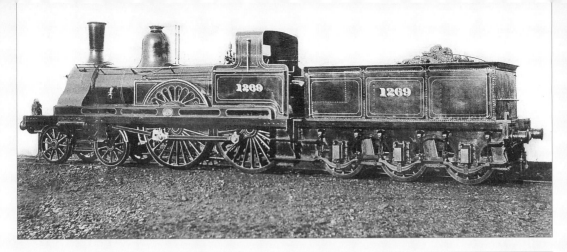

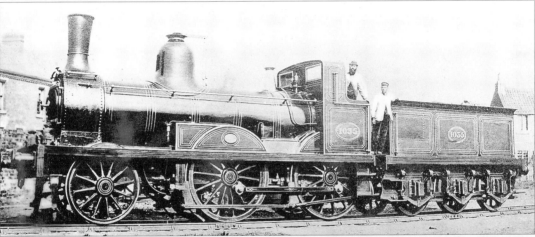

Top:
Bouch's last 4-4-0 was the most unconventional — and the most unsuccessful — of them all. It had several experimental features including brass piston-valves. Ten were built; Mr Bouch retired in 1875 and Edward Fletcher immediately rebuilt the 'Ginx's Babies', as the unreliable '238s' were known by then, into simple 2-4-0s. This is the short-lived No 1269 when new in 1874. *Locomotive Publishing Co/Ian Allan Library*

Above:
Between 1875 and 1882 14 passenger locomotives in three classes were the last dedicated S&DR engines. All were conventional 2-4-0s and portrayed typical Fletcher lineage. No 1035 was one of the six members of the 1875 '1068' or 'Gamecock' class. They did not carry individual names but apparently earned their class name from their agility over Stainmore. *Locomotive Publishing Co/Ian Allan Library*

Overleaf, top:
A bewildering variety of locomotives was built by the NER and its constituents throughout the 19th century.

No 40 of Class 40 was the first of the last four S&DR locomotives built in 1882 at Darlington Works. No longer confined to the Tees, No 40 is immaculate at York and about to head Teeswards, at the turn of the century. *Locomotive Publishing Co/Ian Allan Library*

Overleaf, centre:
The top-link 'Tennants' also finished their days in humble but hard work over Stainmore. This fine study of No 1477 and crew recovering at Darlington after arrival from Penrith in May 1927 shows the 'born-again Fletcher' lines characteristic of No 40 illustrated previously, after McDonnell's brief 'lean lines' intervention. *J. E. Kite*

Overleaf, bottom:
The crew are obviously proud of their smart 'BTP'. Fletcher's 'Bogie Tank Passenger' 0-4-4 well tanks were built between 1874 and 1883 with a bewildering variety of cylinder and coupled-wheel sizes and the many typical Fletcher 'detail differences'. This is No 1346, built by Hawthorn in 1875. *Locomotive Publishing Co/Ian Allan Library*

3. One Railway

The North Eastern Railway was formed less than 30 years after the inauguration of the S&DR in 1825 when the latter was a mainly horse-drawn public toll railway, dedicated principally to the haulage of coal from pit to port. By 1854 the NER had fulfilled Joseph Pease's vision of 1835 in its formation of a vital link with the Great Northern and North British railways to form the East Coast trunk railway which ran from London to Edinburgh. It carried people at 60mph in comfortable, braked and heated corridor coached trains, hauled by powerful passenger-dedicated steam locomotives; all this in stark contrast to the jolting, unbraked, four-wheeled vehicles which had slowly traversed the S&DR in the 1830s — and which had surprised the S&DR committee with their popularity. The worth of the steam locomotive-hauled passenger train had finally been proved in 1829 by the Rainhill locomotive trials and the ensuing opening of the Liverpool & Manchester Railway (L&MR). From the L&MR a web of small railways spread north and south, finally, in 1846, to form the London & North Western Railway which, with the Caledonian, from 1847 formed the West Coast trunk route from London to Glasgow.

These West and East Coast trunk lines were the largest conglomerates in a general nationwide 'post-mania' synthesis of smaller lines into large, integrated inter-city systems. Directors of neigh-bouring railways now often sought co-operation rather than competition in order to secure best results, while, through constant dispute and reconciliation, they now worked towards improved industrial relationships with their employees. The amalgamations and takeovers seen daily in today's 'new technologies' are somewhat reminiscent of this synthesis of the emerging 19th century railway system, while the final 20th century achievement of one nationwide railway system has today, with sad irony, been broken back into smaller, competing units, often with most unfortunate results.

In 1854, the pioneer, east-west lines which had started this great transport revolution on Teesside remained, for the time being, independent. Teesside boomed. Coal and iron ore came into the area virtually non-stop in order to feed the multiplying blast furnaces and coke ovens from which a stream of iron ingots, prepared coke and associated products were worked away. By 1857, C. J. Allen tells us there were 'as many furnaces in blast on Teesside . . . as there had been in the whole of Durham and Northumberland' in 1850.

As the S&DR and Hartlepool railways scrambled to keep pace with this ever-increasing demand, they became involved in a new round of competition which escalated from the 'War of the Three Rivers' into the perhaps inevitable 'War of the Giants' between the new East and West Coast routes.

The completion of the SD&LUR and its north-western links in 1861/2 opened the North East to the designs of the LNWR which had long objected to the carriage of its eastbound goods via Normanton (Lancashire & Yorkshire Railway), rather than by its own lines. The LNWR now saw the booming prosperity across the Pennines and sought shares in the new North Eastern bounty. On Teesside, the LNWR went so far as to purchase £100,000 worth of warehousing in West Hartlepool in preparation for its presumptive arrival in the new port. The WHH&R, of course, encouraged this, but by 1860 it was in serious financial difficulties, soon to be exacerbated by the Ward Jackson scandal.

Benjamin Coleman was a stockbroker to whom Ralph Ward Jackson's brother Edwin became indebted, and it was Ralph's attempts to extricate his brother which led to Coleman's determination to extract his pound of flesh from the Ward Jackson family. The technical illegalities which Coleman uncovered — Ward Jackson had used railway revenue to safeguard company shipping interests — resulted in the unfortunate Ralph Ward Jackson's resignation in 1862, in similar circumstances to those of George Hudson in 1849.

The financial implications of the Ward Jackson scandal provided reinforcement for the NER.

For amalgamation was now inevitable for the WHH&R, the LNWR's gateway into Teesside, while the old S&DR's committee, caught between two young giants, also realised that it could no longer compete in this new and expanding railway world. The S&DR chose the neighbour to which it had shown the way, rather than the alien from over the hills, and became part of the NER in 1863 — with provisos that a Darlington committee operate the pioneer line and also the Stockton quays independently for 10 years. The amalgamation bought off the S&DR's involvement with the LNWR's intended Derwent Valley route into Tyneside, and with the WHH&R's formal amalgamation in 1865 the LNWR's access to the North East was finally closed.

With the absorption of other lines further south, the NER now included every independent railway between the Humber and the Tyne, and with over 1,200 route miles and the coal and iron of Durham and Teesside had become one of the most influential railways in the country. The bold attempts at invasion from outside had but

resulted in the defensive North Eastern alliances and amalgamations which ultimately brought together erstwhile competitors into 'the most complete monopoly in the UK' (Irving).

R. J. Irving saw the railway years to 1866 as years of 'construction', characterised by inter-company competition, while from 1866 until 1914 growth continued 'in response to the needs of trade and industry'. These latter years were of 'the first stage of the age of operation'. During the transitional years between 'construction' and 'operation' (or, better, 'consolidation'), 'production rose at a rate that astonished the world' (Checkland). Durham coal production soared by 15 million tons, almost equal to the total production of the rest of the world and representing the total national output in 1816. Iron production, coal's 'instrumental twin', as Checkland called it, rose from 4 million to 5 million tons between 1862 and 1865, and by 1875 Cleveland produced and processed one third of the kingdom's output. Teesside and Cleveland were thus directly responsible for the NER's continuing premier position among railways during the economic troughs which periodically furrowed Britain's 19th century industry.

In 1867, the NER's attempts to balance receipts with workers' demands and rising prices were upset by a barrister and shareholder by the name of Henry Trotter who claimed that the NER was skimping on maintenance in order to pay higher dividends. He compared NER with GNR figures

Below:
A smart two-year-old Standard '4MT' tank, No 80117 of Whitby, stands in Stockton station in April 1956 with a Yorkshire coast train. The station was built after the arrival of the ambitious Leeds Northern Railway and the resulting formation of the North Eastern Railway in the mid-1850s. *J. Davenport/N. Stead collection*

Above:
In August 1937, one of 190 old faithful 'J25' (NER 'P1') 0-6-0s, No 1979, ambles across the main line at the S&DR level crossing and heads for North Road and the Aucklands. *J. W. Armstrong*

in support of this accusation — prophetically similar to that made in 2000. The company demonstrated that its accounting procedure differed from that of the GNR and, although it was quickly exonerated, the actions of this one misguided man cost the company a £750,000 fall in share value. Henry Trotter can be seen as another Benjamin Coleman, but his victim was a much bigger organisation, and while his intentions were honest, they contributed towards the loss of some £1,000,000 in NER gross receipts between 1875 and 1879. Indeed, by 1879, with receipts down on all traffic and the miners on strike in both Northumberland and Durham, NER income reached its lowest ebb with share dividends at 5%, half the 1873 yield.

The increasing output of the Durham coalfield before 1879 and the insatiable demand on Teesside for iron and steel and their finished products, however, saw the North Eastern Railway through this difficult period. The same demands at a time of fluctuating prices and unemployment during the 1870s turned the slowly accelerating drift of immigrant workers to the North East into a flood as new agricultural methods and the latest economic depression brought unemployment to the South of England and to Wales; even so, the demand for miners could not always be met. As in the 1840s, Teesside and northern industry provided timely employment for the redundant British worker within its own island of industrial prosperity. This northern Utopia would not last for ever.

Above:
In August 1937, one of 190 old faithful 'J25' (NER 'P1') 0-6-0s, No 1979, ambles across the main line at the S&DR level crossing and heads for North Road and the Aucklands. *J. W. Armstrong*

Despite the economic uncertainties of the 1870s, the NER was obliged to address the steadily growing congestion in the approaches to Teesside. On the old Clarence route, coal trains converged at Stillington and queued for access through Norton Junction to Haverton Hill and Port Clarence, while S&DR traffic had to cross the East Coast main line on the level at Darlington, merge with iron-ore trains at Preston Junction (now Eaglescliffe), then vie with them for a path through to Middlesbrough. North-south traffic, freight to and from Teesside, and through passenger workings via Stockton on the old Leeds Northern route to Hartlepool, cut and joined these west to east routes at both Norton and Preston junctions. Room had also to be found throughout for the frequent local passenger trains running between the growing Teesside settlements. In 1863, a first attempt to ease the situation involved the addition of a curve from Bowesfield Junction northwest to connect with the Leeds Northern line at Hartburn Junction, south of Stockton (LNR) station. Hartburn curve enabled trains from the Clarence route to travel via Stockton into Middlesbrough (unthinkable a decade earlier!) and constituted the first link in an extremely busy junction complex.

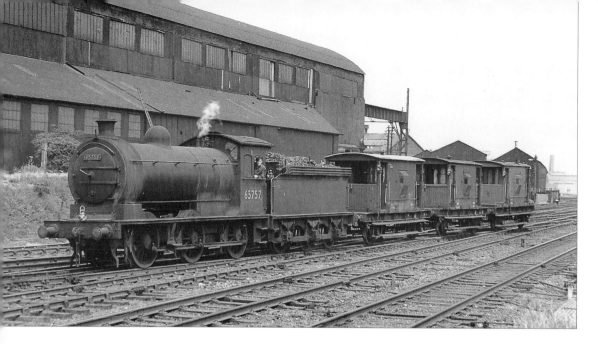

Thornaby depot's 'J26' 0-6-0 No 65757 has Bowesfield Junction to itself as it leaves the main line and crosses with three brake vans in June 1959. This is the Bowesfield which grew from the initial 1863 curve. Up and down main lines between Darlington and Teesside are nearest the camera while the original S&DR route to the passenger terminus and Stockton Wharf turns left, furthest from the camera, behind the train. In 1830 the new Middlesbrough branch turned right at this point. The layout eventually accommodated the 1877 extension to the Castle Eden branch, which No 65757 is just crossing, to take the 1863 relief curve round to Hartburn Junction, Stockton and Norton. *K. Hoole/N. Stead collection*

In 1865, Carlton Ironworks was opened near remote Stillington and soon grew into a thriving township with its own Carlton Ironworks station — and a further increase in the teeming Teesside traffic. The first steps towards formal marshalling arrangements were made at Shildon in 1869, and by the mid-1870s 'laden' and 'empties' yards stood each side of the passenger lines between Shildon and Middridge, while much of the Clarence line was quadrupled between Stillington and Carlton. Middlesbrough dock was enlarged in 1874, while one year later the first dedicated marshalling yard at Newport, just west of Middlesbrough, was opened. Built on level, reclaimed marshland, this was one of the earliest gravity-assisted hump sorting yards. In 1881, Newport locomotive shed was added to the complex, only to be resited and enlarged in 1890 after subsidence.

The increase in Middlesbrough's passenger traffic was recognised by a new station, opened in 1877. This year also saw the opening of the southern section of the Castle Eden branch relieving line, which, on completion in 1878, enabled Durham coal traffic to run directly south, 12 miles, from a junction with the old HD&R line at Castle Eden North (Wellfield) into Teesside. Connections at Wingate and Wellfield with the ex-GNE,C&HJR route to Ferryhill and further south at Carlton, with the old Clarence line, created considerable junction complexes at both locations. From the extremely busy Carlton and Norton junctions, traffic to and from Newport Yard was funnelled through Bowesfield Junction, as was traffic to from the south via Preston Junction, which would later become Eaglescliffe.

Eastwards from Teesside, difficult engineering on the extension of the S&DR line, started in 1866 and known as the Whitby, Redcar & Middlesbrough Union Railway, resulted in financial difficulties, and the NER took over construction in 1875. Operations commenced in 1883.

West of Darlington the NER made two similar acquisitions at this time. The Forcett Railway of 1866 and the Merrybent & Darlington of 1870 which ran south to serve stone quarries. Initially

Above:
The Standard '9Fs' were BR's last steam locomotive type and were extremely successful — and unexpectedly versatile. None was allocated to Teesside sheds but Tyne Dock had 10, most of which regularly worked up to Tees Yard. Here No 92061 has come through Norton Junction and Stockton and now heads into the 1863 curve to Bowesfield Junction and Tees Yard at Hartburn Junction. *K. Hoole/N. Stead collection*

independent, both were soon taken over by the NER, as was the Tees Valley Railway, opened in 1868 to serve stone quarries out at Middleton-in-Teesdale, whence stone was transported to Barnard Castle and then, inevitably, into the insatiable maw of Teesside.

These years of final 'construction' and new 'consolidation' saw the rebuilding of Bishop Auckland station into its final platformed triangle in 1867 while, 10 years later, major dock reconstruction in the 'far east' at Hartlepool provided a new and permanent north-south line running west around the docks in place of the earlier, more easterl, S&HR / HD&R routes. West Hartlepool's new station was opened in 1880, replacing two S&HR predecessors. Five years later, despite a fall in shipbuilding iron and steel requirements and a corresponding steep fall in NER profits during 1884, the Byers Green branch was extended from Spennymoor to Bishop Auckland, uniting that town with Hartlepool and building the third station at Byers Green, whose railway history is surely as complex as many a larger railway junction town.

In the midst of the busy, contradictory 1870s, the S&DR Jubilee was celebrated at Darlington. *Locomotion* was exhibited together with a cavalcade of locomotives illustrating the amazing advances which had been made in railway and locomotive development through that first brief half-century of public railways. In 1875, hundreds of second-generation six-wheelers, successors to

Timothy Hackworth's *Royal George*, constantly trundled freight and minerals through congested Teesside alongside Edward Fletcher's nimble new four-coupled 'bogie' tank engines which worked the frequent local passenger trains, while his '901' class 2-4-0s looked after the NER's portion of the East Coast main line express trains. The S&DR Jubilee is an event which has celebrated the unique revolution in transport, industry and the railway each quarter-century since — until August 2000, when many millions of pounds were doomed in a vain display of new-millennium technology while history and tradition were abandoned for the lack of a few thousand pounds.

A new burden was placed on the railway companies in 1894 when increasing complaints from traders realised the Railway Act, standard-ising a 70-year proliferation of freight charges which were often different for the same commodity carried by different operators over

Left:
'V1' 2-6-2T No 7669 (NER No 451) was in the station at the time of the air raid in August 1942 and was subsequently in need of fitters' attention.
Ian Allan Library

the same routes, and now continued by the new conglomerates. Freight-dependent railways such as the NER were particularly disadvantaged by the new standard rates, but railways and, indeed, industry in general were now set in a constant struggle to balance a viable income, in a Britain no longer the leader in world industry, against effective industrial relations with a workforce constantly and justifiably seeking shorter working hours and better working conditions. This inevitably increased the expenses of even the most indulgent companies. The NER led the way in railway industrial relations in 1889 when it agreed to arbitration during a dispute with the Amalgamated Society of Railway Servants, while, in 1890, it became the first company to agree to conduct all future negotiations through trade union representatives. This agreement is

still recognised today, in technology's family language as 'dumbed-down Industrial Relations'.

Against this controversial economic background Teesside's railways worked on — the NER's 'cutting edge'. In 1882, Castle Eden North Junction was renamed simply Wellfield, while the ongoing fight with congestion included more mineral lines at the western approaches to Newport Yard. This necessitated the building of a new station at South Stockton, while some three years later the quadruple roads between Stillington and Carlton West Junction were relaid in such a way that trains from Shildon could run from Stillington in parallel with trains from Ferryhill, as far as Carlton West Junction. Stillington — ex-Carlton Ironworks — and Carlton stations were rebuilt as islands to accommodate the new formation.

Above:
The west to north curve completed the station triangle at Bishop Auckland in 1867 and had but one 'inside' platform which was seldom used by regular passenger services. However, the photogenic Thompson 'L1' 2-6-4T No 67777 of Darlington was caught running in from the Crook direction sometime in the early 1950s bearing Class A lamps and an excursion number. The train is believed to be one of the by then rare and under-exploited 'football excursions'; Willington, Crook and Bishop Auckland were all in the Northern Amateur League. The two mature 'fans' on the platform are pointedly not interested in 'all the sevens'! In the background, the 1842 west–east 'main line' runs in front of the signalbox and into the single platform on the base of the triangle, where eastbound trains had to turn in.
J. W. Armstrong

On 6 October 1892 South Stockton became the Borough of Thornaby. As a result, the rebuilt 1882 S&DR South Stockton station became 'Thornaby', while the LNR/WHH&R North Stockton station became just 'Stockton'. Just beyond Bowesfield and over the S&DR's 1830 crossing of the Tees, Thornaby stands at the western entry to Teesside's huge marshalling yards, which have changed shape and name several times since 1875. All traffic approaching the yards from the west must bypass Thornaby station and for many years the procession was virtually non-stop. Stockton and Middlesbrough were now essentially three boroughs. Not until 1968 were Stockton and Middlesbrough amalgamated to form an 'official' Teesside – one drastically different from that recalled by Joseph Pease in a reminiscence made in 1863 when, he remembered, 'the silence and solitude of . . . this part of the Tees were only broken by the presence of a few grey-headed seals and a few shrimping women' (Tomlinson). A complete rebuild of the layout at Carlton station in 1895 remodelled Carlton West Junction and was the last big 19th century Teesside railway alteration.

The dawn of the 20th century found Teesside yet busier with a great diversity of traffic apart from the eternal coal and ore conveyed in new high-capacity wagons from 1901. The manufacturing processes of the finished iron and steel products in turn produced by-products often with their own utility: coke itself, chemicals and even blast furnace slag with uses in such diverse manufactures as fertilizers and road stone. There was also salt from a very busy brine processing plant centred upon Port Clarence, flour and offal from a mill at Stockton,

and copper ore and barytes coming east from Durham and North Yorkshire, while Durham was surpassed only by Lanark in its production of fireclay. After its shortfall in the 1880s the shipbuilding industry developed to such an extent in the new century that new yards were opened at Haverton Hill and Hartlepool.

All this — and empties to serve all, together with the ubiquitous passenger traffic — had to pass through the three 'doorways' into Teesside, all now controlled by modern block signalling. By 1905, however, marshalling arrangements had again become inadequate and in 1907 work commenced on a new yard west of (and linked by three bridges across the tributary Old Tees to) the 1875 Newport Yard. The new complex was opened on 14 December 1908 and named Erimus Yard after Middlesbrough's town motto — 'We shall be'. Erimus Yard included both up and down 'hump' facilities and virtually doubled the total Newport wagon capacity. In 1910, the first ever railway area control office was opened in the midst of Erimus Yard. 'Control' monitored the whole vast conglomeration of Teesside and Cleveland railway operations and set the precedent for a national system.

Across the estuary, the increasing importance of the Hartlepools at the turn of the 19th century saw the diversion of through passenger trains between Newcastle and the South via Sunderland and Stockton from the Wellfield route in order to serve West Hartlepool, which gained two more platforms in 1907. Teesside's last through line was opened in 1905 along the coast from Hartlepool to Seaham and Ryhope where the Wellfield route was regained into Sunderland. Sanctioned in 1894/5, this new coast line was 3¼ miles longer than via Wellfield. However, it avoided the 1 in 44 Ryhope Bank southbound and the 1 in 52 Hesleden northwards.

NER LOCOMOTIVES ON TEESSIDE:
THE WORSDELLS AND VINCENT RAVEN

Above:
Thomas Worsdell (T. W.), was appointed CME of the NER in 1885. Both Thomas and Wilson Worsdell had worked under Francis Webb at Crewe on the LNWR, although Thomas came to the NER from the GER. His first North Eastern engine perpetuated his last Great Eastern type in the neat shape of the Class A (LNER/BR Class F8) 2-4-2 passenger tank. T. W.'s classification was the first attempt to bring order to future NER locomotive design. The previous proliferation was (and still is!) beyond redemption. The 'letter' classification was carried, not ideally, into the 20th century by Vincent Raven. No 172 was built at the NER's Gateshead Works in 1888. *Locomotive Publishing Co/Ian Allan Library*

Below:
In 1886, T. W. Worsdell produced his first 0-6-0 goods locomotive, although with 5ft 1in wheels they proved to be extremely useful and long-lived mixed-traffic engines. As new they successfully worked the NE's main line freight trains, between Newcastle and York. Class C used the Worsdell-von Borries compound system, while the simple version was known as Class C1. Over 200 were built up to 1895. 'C1' No 1811 still looks brand-new in ex-works black after coming over Stainmore to Darlington as BR Class J21 No 65119 in 1950. *E. D. Bruton*

Top right:
Classes B and B1 (LNER/BR Class N8) were respectively compound and simple 0-6-2 tank versions of the 'Cs'. Members of both simple types lasted well into BR days, although No 855 — seen here when new — was withdrawn before LNER re-numbering in 1946. *Ian Allan Library*

Lower right:
Another long-lived — and long-built — design was the six-coupled 0-6-0T of Classes E (4ft 6in) and E1 (4ft wheels). A total of 120 'Es' (LNER Class J71) were built between 1886 and 1895, while 75 neat 'E1s' (LNER/BR 'J72') were constructed between 1898 and 1922. These were topped up with 10 more in 1925 and added to yet again by BR who built no fewer than 29 in 1949-51 at Doncaster, 50 years after the first of the class! No 581 was the first of the 1925 batch and is seen in its grey 'photographic livery' as new.
Locomotive Publishing Co/Ian Allan Library

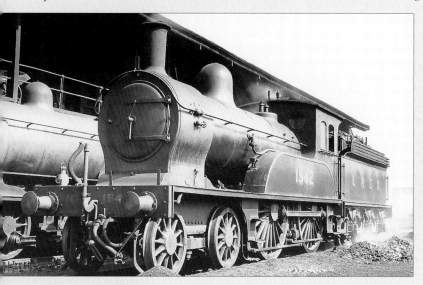

Left:
Compound 'F' class and simple 'F1s' were T. Worsdell's first and extremely successful 4-4-0 express engines in 1887. When new they were, literally, East Coast racing engines and did not live on Teesside until their later years. West Hartlepool shed always had several 'big old engines' for the coast route trains to Sunderland and Newcastle. Thus, handsome 6ft 8in 'F1'(LNER 'D22') No 1542 stands on West Hartlepool's ash pits in June 1932 towards the end of some 40 years' service. *Ian Allan Library*

Right:
Outside West Hartlepool shed, all of 22 years later, stand two examples of T. Worsdell's last class, the 'Ls', an uprated 'E' 0-6-0T. Built in 1891/2, Nos 547 (BR No 68358) and 553 (68364) were ready to go to work in April 1954 when all 10 members of the class were still active as BR 'J73s'.
T. K. Widd

Right:
In 1894, the 'O' class 0-4-4T appeared as worthy successor to the Fletcher 'BTPs' and was soon at work throughout the NER. No 7262 (NER No 1865) is 'disposed' on an unidentified ash pit in LNER days.
Ian Allan Library

Left:
Also in 1894, the next NER examples of the eternal 0-6-0 locomotive emerged. Classes P and P1 were developments of Class C1, but with 4ft 7in wheels were essentially goods engines. No 1891 (LNER No 5620) was one of the 70 'Ps' built up to 1898. Built until 1903, 120 'P1s' followed the 'Ps', the LNER making them Classes J24 and J25.
Ian Allan Library

Above:
The NER opened the new century with the massive 'S' class, the first British passenger 4-6-0, intended for work outside Teesside. The new 'big engine' policy continued in 1901 with the mighty 'T' class eight-coupled goods engine. The 'Ts' had piston valves and the 'T1s' ordinary slide valves. No 2122 (LNER No 3256) of the first batch of 'Ts' is seen when new. In all, 90 'T' and 'T1' 0-8-0s (both LNER Class Q5) were built through to 1911. *Real Photos*

Below:
Class P2 was clearly no relation of the earlier 'Ps'. The 'P2' continued the 'big engine' policy by carrying a 5ft 6in diameter boiler on an 0-6-0 chassis. All 50 of this stocky class (LNER 'J26') were built 1904/5 and eventually allocated to Newport shed. Many of the 115-strong, detail-difference 'P3s' (LNER 'J27') constructed over almost two decades from 1906 were also allocated to Teesside depots and were *the* 'everyday' 0-6-0 until the end of steam in the area. No 1678 (LNER No 5748) was an early 'P2' and is depicted in NER days complete with Fletcher-type brass safety-valve cover.

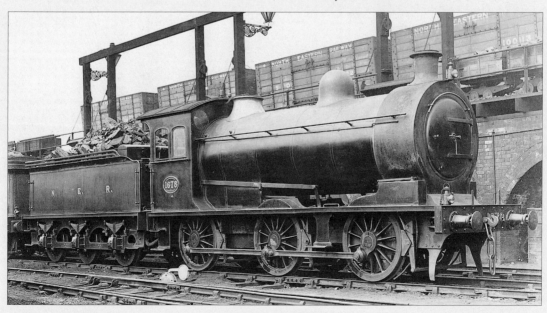

Above:
'W' can be said to be for 'Whitby' when the big engines included a 5ft 1¼in-driving wheel 4-6-0 tank design for that hilly route eastwards from Middlesbrough in 1907. The magnificent 'Whitby Tanks' needed more coal and a bigger bunker later which saw them converted to 4-6-2Ts. In this guise, No 687 is seen in LNER days as LNER 'A6' class No 9791. *Ian Allan Library*

Below:
'X' marked the spot when the 'big tank' turned up as eight-coupled and with three cylinders in the new Erimus Yard. Ten 4-8-0T Class Xs were built in 1909/10 for hump shunting. They were the last engines completed at Gateshead Works, all further locomotive construction taking place at Darlington where five more 'Xs' (LNER 'T1') were built in 1925 for other LNER yards. No 1352 is in photographic grey in 1909. It later became LNER No 9912. *Locomotive Publishing Co/Ian Allan Library*

Above:
The last letter of T. W. Worsdell's alphabetical classification was applied to Vincent Raven's excellent three-cylinder express 4-4-2 which joined Wilson Worsdell's equally successful 'Vs' on the East Coast main line in 1911. 'Z' class No 706 was the first Raven Atlantic, and in her heyday probably only saw the Tees at the Croft crossing. In 1945, however, she was found in a very sad condition on Newport shed. Now LNER Class C7, she was renumbered 2950 before withdrawal by 1948. *Ian Allan Library*

Below:
Raven continued the big three-cylinder tank engine type with Class D (unused in the earlier classification) 4-4-4T for passenger haulage on longer branches and the North Yorkshire coast lines. To improve adhesion, all 45 LNER 'H1s' were rebuilt as 'A8' class 4-6-2Ts from 1931. No 2143, the first 'D', built in 1913, is shown in 1921 when carrying a third-rail electricity pick-up shoe which was feasibility-tested on the Yorkshire coast line curves with a view to using that system on the projected East Coast electrification. *Ian Allan Library*

Right:
BR No 69863 — a fine example of the very successful 'D' conversion — the big 'A8' 4-6-2T is seen ready for action on her home shed, West Hartlepool, on 17 May 1952. *R. E. Vincent*

Below right:
Before these conversions were carried out, Nigel Gresley ordered a batch of 13 Robinson GCR 1911-design inside cylinder '9N' class 4-6-2Ts in 1925 specifically to work the Middlesbrough to Whitby line — although No 9811, found at Darlington in June 1950, is a GCR 'original' (No 451) and later returned to Hull. These 'foreign' 'horses for courses' continued to work alongside the 'A8s' and LNER Thompson 'L1' class 2-6-4Ts until the end. *E. D. Bruton*

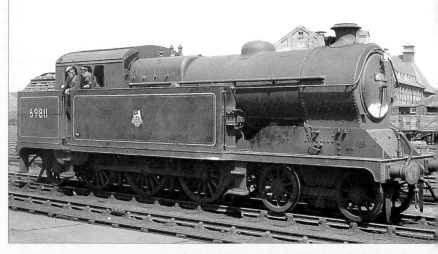

Below:
While the 'P2s' and 'P3s' had no affinity with the 'Ps' and 'P1s', Raven's superheated 'T2' of 1913 was clearly descended from the 1901 'T'. These fine 0-8-0s joined the 'P2'/'P3' 0-6-0s as the most familiar LNER Teesside mineral engines. Both types comprised a simple, free-steaming design, 'capable of being worked all out', said C. J. Allen, 'even at around 70% cut-off with wide-open regulator, over quite appreciable distances'. Seen in 1913 in photographic grey is brand-new No 1247 (LNER No 3340), the first of the 120 'T2s' built up until 1921 and which became LNER 'Q6' class. *Locomotive Publishing Co/Ian Allan Library*

4. War Railways

In 1902, Tyneside Tramways started an immediately popular electric tram service between Gosforth and North Shields. Two years later, a similar scheme on the far side of the Pennines linked Liverpool with Southport, and such projects marked the beginning of the road transport renaissance which would take off in the 1920s and eventually reverse the rail revolution of a century before. The 1902 threat was seen off with the NER electrification of Newcastle suburban rail services and the difficult quayside branch. The success of this project and a visit to the USA by Vincent Raven, the NER's new Chief Mechanical Engineer, led to the decision to electrify a main line on an experimental basis. There is some irony in the fact that the old and disputed Clarence 'direct' line, now with its regular heavy coal traffic from Shildon into Erimus Yard via its diversion through Carlton and Bowesfield junctions, was chosen for this most ambitious project. Partial operation commenced on 1 July 1915, despite the outbreak of World War 1, with three of the fleet of 10 Bo-Bo electric locomotives, designed and built at Darlington Works, working nights between Middridge and Bowesfield. Throughout electric haulage on the line started early in 1917.

But 1913 proved to be the culmination of railway development on Teesside, or indeed, of forward British railway progress altogether. It was not only the end of Irving's 'years of consolidation' but truly the end of an era. For, while rail traffic thrived during the first decade of the century, economic growth nationally fell by some 50% as other countries, notably Germany and the USA, began to build their own industrial societies. From 1914, some 30 'war years' served to cushion the world's first industrial power's railways from the blow dealt to them as emerging nations stood alone and as the old heavy industries gradually gave way to new, light industries and new technology.

Upon the outbreak of World War 1, all railways were taken over by the Government and given into the charge of the Railway Executive Committee under the President of the Board of Trade. To all intents and purposes they were nationalised for the duration.

Right:
The new century introduced new 'big engines' to the NER. In 1906 comparative trials were run over Stainmore between piston-valved 'T' class 0-8-0 No 2125 and slide-valve 'T1' sister No 130. Both easily worked 25 loaded mineral wagons, brake van and dynamometer car without assistance. No 130 gave the best results, but weight restrictions no doubt prevented regular use of these big engines which could have introduced single-engine freight working on the route. Here, No 2125 is ready to leave Kirkby Stephen with a test trip back to Darlington.
Ian Allan Library

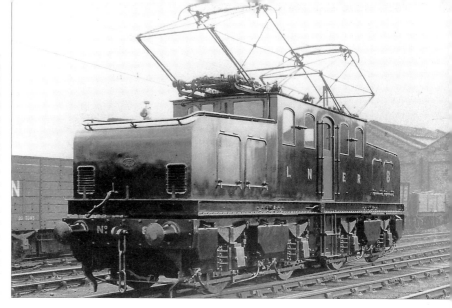

Right:
Raven's ambitious Shildon to Erimus electrification commenced in 1915. Ten Bo-Bo locomotives were built at Darlington for the new service, numbered 3-12. The engine used in the 1921 electric versus steam trials which increased train weights from 1,000 to 1,400 tons, No 8, waits menacingly at Shildon in LNER days. *Darlington*

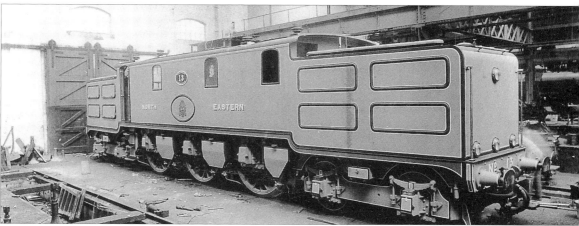

Above:
In 1920, Sir Vincent Raven's visionary plan for East Coast main line electrification was still so probable that the first electric express locomotive was tested on the Clarence line. No 13 was a 4-6-4 (or 2-Co-2) and was carried on driving wheels of 6ft 8in express steam diameter! Eventually finished in LNER green, it is seen here in Darlington Works in photographic livery when brand-new in 1922 — a grey predator from the future . . . *K. L. Taylor Collection/Darlington*

From 1914, Teesside railways, forged in the commercial wars which had eventually brought them together as essential components of the NER, played their part in the transport of troops and materials, and in the compulsory loan of their own equipment, during a real and dreadful worldwide war. In 1918, exhausted and run down, they looked forward to a return to prewar prosperity, and for a short while this renaissance appeared to be a distinct probability despite constant unrest within the workforce. Vincent Raven returned to the NER in 1919 with a wartime knighthood and immediately turned his attention to the prewar electrification project. No 13 emerged from Darlington Works in 1922, a new electric passenger locomotive built on the lines of the Shildon freighters — but with 6ft 8in driving wheels! This locomotive was to run on the proposed electrified main line between York and Newcastle, thus anticipating the Class 91s by more than half a century!

During 1920, however, even traditional coal and iron traffic declined as the postwar British boom suddenly turned to depression. The North

Eastern main line electrification scheme was dropped in the face of declining traffic. By the winter of 1921/2 over 2 million were unemployed throughout the land in 'one of the worst years of depression since the industrial revolution'. (Quoted from the *Economist,* by A. J. P. Taylor.) It was under this fast-approaching shadow of economic collapse that the new Ministry of Transport decided, conveniently, that Britain's railways would be returned to private ownership, but that they must be 'rationalised' in the modern manner and formed into larger, 'more efficient' units. Under the 1921 Railways Act, Teesside's railways, as components of the North Eastern Railway, became part of the North Eastern Area of the London & North Eastern Railway (LNER), the second-largest of the new 'Big Four' railway companies: the London, Midland & Scottish Railway (LMS), LNER, Great Western Railway (GWR) and Southern Railway (SR).

In 1923, the Act became law and while Lord Joicey, last Deputy Chairman of the NER, referred to the 'very splendid property' which the NER bequeathed to its parent LNER with reserves of £10 million, he also had to admit to a traffic decline of 22% in freight and 14% in passenger traffic during 1921/2.

At this time, the NER was also in dispute with the Newcastle Electric Supply Co over its electricity bill for both Tyneside and Teesside. The Tyneside equipment was now 20 years old and due for renewal, while the worsening depression in the national economy and consequent failure in mineral traffic finally brought about the cessation of electric traction on the Shildon–Newport line at the end of 1934.

The disastrous depression decimated the nation, resulting in unemployment levels not seen since those early railway days, the 'Hungry Forties'. On Teesside, North Stockton Yard closed in 1930, while 1932 saw Shildon Yard working just one shift before closing completely in 1934, by which time traffic was one seventh of 1913 levels. Steam traction had resumed on the old Clarence route, although Shildon locomotive depot was closed in 1935. The Newport and Erimus yards were 'rationalised' from 1931. By 1936, three distinct marshalling yards had been formed out of the Erimus layout and, significantly, the ambitious Erimus title was dropped; perhaps it should have been retained, slightly amended, as 'Eramus' — 'We were'!

No more now would North Eastern industry welcome the unemployed from more depressed parts of the country. The local economy never really recovered from this period and high unemployment became the norm, as also on fellow railway pioneer Merseyside, across the Pennines.

The only prosperity on interwar Teesside was at Imperial Chemical Industries, a product of wartime research which opened in Billingham

as the Synthetic Ammonia & Nitrate Co in 1918. ICI became a working demonstration of the inescapable fact that the coal, coke, iron and steel products were no longer the 'in' industries and they must give way to the new 'technologies', very much based on electricity as well as chemicals and oil-based fuels and the burgeoning motor car industry, established particularly in the south of the country.

The eastward shift of the Durham coalfield also brought about a change in rail traffic patterns around Teesside; the old Auckland field was working out while pits were still being sunk in the east. Thus Fishburn Colliery was a late sinking in the southeast corner of the Durham coalfield. Opened in that halcyon railway year of 1913 when traffic was at its greatest, a branch was thrown off to the colliery from the old Clarence's Durham 'bough' at Bishop Middleham signalbox just ¾ mile north of isolated Sedgefield station, which itself carried a busy livestock traffic for the traditional farming communities of south Durham, thriving south of the coalfield. Industries ancient and modern merged here during Teesside railways' last prosperous years and were the first to experience service reductions during the Depression.

Above:
That first journey from Shildon was re-enacted in September 1925, two years after the Grouping and on the eve of the Depression. *Locomotion*, miraculously petrol-driven from the tender and with oily-rag exhaust, came on from Eaglescliffe with the centenary replica train triumphantly to enter the 1852 Leeds Northern station at Stockton (LNER), 100 years after its first appearance at St John's Crossing. *Ian Allan Library*

Early passenger traffic on the S&DR had exceeded expectations and had grown apace over the years. Developing Teesside was well served by commuter trains and every branch had its local passenger train. Trains connected into long-distance expresses at Darlington, West Hartlepool and Middlesbrough, while excursions at cheap fares had run increasingly since the 1840s as some time off from work was agreed between employers and trade unions. In 1931, however, necessary economies caused the withdrawal of passenger services between Stockton and Wellfield, while Stockton to Ferryhill services were worked by Sentinel steam railcars. Later, in December 1939, services were withdrawn between Bishop Auckland and Spennymoor.

Above:
An express overtakes a train of empty flat wagons on the goods road as it enters Middlesbrough station in 1957. The empties are in the charge of hard-working 'J26' No 65755 while the express is managed by No 61478, one of Sir Vincent Raven's most successful 'S3' mixed traffic 4-6-0s of 1919, LNER 'B16'. None was allocated to Teesside sheds but No 61478 is from 50D, Starbeck, and has worked the train through from Harrogate via the old Leeds Northern main line through Northallerton and Eaglescliffe, a traditional Teesside cross-country connection soon to be discontinued. *G. M. Staddon/N. Stead collection*

Below:
The view towards Simpasture with Demons Bridge box still standing during demolition of the R. O. factory and junction in 1948.
J. W. Armstrong/Darlington

Economic recovery began from mid-decade, while after 1937 the economy was again boosted artificially by the demand for new armaments. On Teesside, Shildon and North Stockton yards reopened in 1939 — and so did hostilities. War was declared on 3 September 1939 and, of course, the railways were again commandeered under the Ministry of Transport's Railway Executive Committee — chaired by Sir Ralph Wedgwood, CEO of the LNER. Traffic immediately increased, and on Teesside the queues to get through Bowesfield were soon as long as ever. In 1944, two more reception roads were provided at Newport, while Shildon became a transit yard for through traffic from the Tyne yards to the south, via Bishop Auckland, Shildon and Darlington. The first public railway lived again, creating a new north-south freight route which relieved the main line to such an extent that it continued to be used until the early 1960s.

As rail-freight increased generally with the onset of war, a local boost was given to Teesside traffic with the opening of a munitions factory near Heighington on the old S&DR line in 1942. An extensive freight reception area, piloted by its own four-wheeled tank engines, was built to cater for Royal Ordnance Factory No 28 while, in anticipation of a daily influx of 30,000 workers (in reality but 12,000 per day!) two new stations were built on spurs from the ex-Clarence main line east of Simpasture Junction. Passenger traffic from Durham via Bishop Auckland terminated at Simpasture station while that from the Teesside direction ran into a station with the

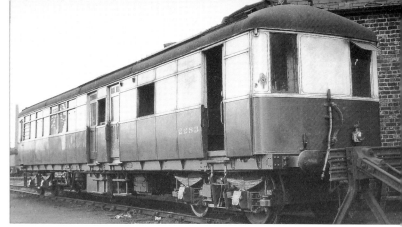

heady name of Demons Bridge — called after the nearby Demons Beck but reminiscent of the days of 'construction' when new embankments were spirited overnight into the Skerne Valley carrs! Trains ran to co-ordinate with shift changes and Demons Bridge trains took their turn in the Teesside traffic east of Stillington.

Aycliffe Royal Ordnance No 28 complex closed with the end of the war in 1945, but it became the nucleus of a new light industrial estate which expanded steadily through the 1950s and '60s into today's considerable, aptly named Newton Aycliffe. It now has its own small station north of old Heighington on the 'World's First Public Railway', just east of the site of Simpasture Junction — a modern monument of new, clean and streamlined industry set on the approaches to the bluff and mucky old industrial Teesland which gave it birth.

Top:
By the mid-1920s, town tramway competition was joined by new, rural road competition as the internal combustion engine offered a more convenient and personal alternative to rail travel. To counter this, railways turned to the steam railcar, using the Sentinel Co's high-pressure, high-speed engine system, all contained within the passenger car. In 1924/5 the LNER tested three chain-driven, two-cylinder railcars and by 1930 had a fleet of 90, mainly geared six-cylinder cars. They worked throughout the Teesside area, from Darlington, around Bishop Auckland, to Middleton-in-Teesdale, and between the Hartlepools. No 2283 *Old Blue* is seen on-shed at Middlesbrough in 1932, when just two years old. It was one of five twin-engined (12-cylinder) 200hp cars built specially for the precipitous Middlesbrough to Whitby and Scarborough line.

Above:
The S&DR line turns sharp right just west of North Road and heads through Heighington and Newton Aycliffe for Shildon. This section of the S&DR still offered a useful alternative East Coast main line diversionary route when 'big engines' could be seen on the 'first railway'. In this c1950 British Railways scene a diverted Edinburgh/Glasgow train passes Heighington behind new Thompson 'A2/3' Pacific No 60516 *Hycilla* which has just crossed the spot where No 1 was assembled some 125 years earlier, having arrived by road in 'kit form' in wagons from the Stephensons' Newcastle Works. Known initially as Aycliffe Lane, Heighington's station buildings were built some years later. *J. W. Armstrong*

LNER LOCOMOTIVES ON TEESSIDE

Above:
On West Hartlepool shed in June 1932 was 1928-built steam railcar No 225 *True Blue*. This was one of 24 chain-drive two-cylinder cars, of Classes D, E and F. No 225 was employed on the shuttle between West and Old Hartlepool. Reported as noisy, rough riding and malodorous, the LNER Sentinel steam railcars survived until 1939. *Ian Allan Library*

Below:
At the Grouping in 1923, Nigel Gresley of the GNR became CME for the entire LNER and his famous locomotives were to serve the whole system, although the NE Section was left much to its own resources. Of his 289 big 'standard' 'J39' class 5ft 2in 0-6-0s, only a few were allocated to Teesside sheds. Built at Darlington between 1926 and 1941 (as well as some by Beyer Peacock in 1936/7) they carried the 'NE look' throughout the LNER. Here, BR No 64835 stands on Thornaby shed in May 1960. *D. J. Dippie*

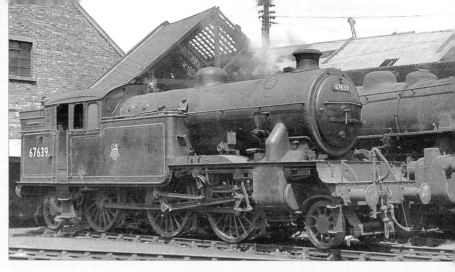

Right:
Apart from the solitary
'A3' Pacific which always
stood main-line pilot at
Darlington, the only other
Gresley engines to grace
Teesside sheds were the
inevitably elegant
'V1'/'V3' 2-6-2Ts of the
1930s. Doncaster-built,
these tanks all served
in the North East and
Scotland. No 67639 was
on Middlesbrough shed
on 13 June 1954.
B. W. L. Brooksbank

Above:
Sir Nigel's conjugated three-cylinder complications
were followed by wartime austerity and the economic
simplicity of Edward Thompson. A total of 409 6ft 2in
diameter driving wheel utility 'B1' 'Antelopes' were
built after 1942, including Stockton's No 1018 which
sported the shortest nameplate ever — *Gnu*.

In October 1948, *Gnu* 'guests' across the river at
Newport in 'weathered' LNER livery, evidently
overdue for an extended visit to Darlington Works.
Several of Thompson's 1949 5ft 2in 'K1' class 2-6-0s,
outwardly similar to the 'B1s', were also at Stockton
for main line goods work. *Ian Allan Library*

Right:
After 1945, several of
Thompson's 100 big two-
cylinder 'L1' class 2-6-4
tanks came to Darlington
and Middlesbrough,
sending the sleek 'V1s'
and 'V3s' north. The
'Concrete Mixers' had but
5ft 2in coupled wheels,
allegedly useful on the
Saltburn line and, while
capable engines, were
prone to new-design
problems. 'All the sevens',
BR No 67777, poses
outside its home shed,
Darlington (51A).
Ian Allan Library

5. Declining Railways

Newton Aycliffe and its New Town peers nationwide are products of the postwar acceleration into new manufacturing methods, 1960s affluence and inflation, and the subsequent and ongoing attempts to slow and control this supersonic conversion of industry into technology. The railways have not come well out of this colossal spin-off from the revolution which they pioneered, and by the 'prosperous '60s', British Railways was by no means sharing in that prosperity. It had, in fact, entered the 'years of decline', when much of the great railway system, which Teesside had pioneered and nurtured as industry's prime mover throughout the preceding 130 and more years, was slowly ignored, choked and then dismembered.

After World War 2, the eastward drift of the Durham field continued, now accompanied by iron and steel which moved away from Middlesbrough's sadly redundant 'rustbelt' (to quote Hobsbawm in *The Age of Extremes*) towards the big, new-process steel foundries around Redcar. This eastward concentration on the larger collieries and specialist steel manufactories represented the final stand of the 'old industries' whose survival now depended on nationalisation, the ultimate move in the postwar social policies of the first strong Labour Government. The coal industry was vested into the National Coal Board on the first day of 1947 and transport followed one year later.

On 1 January 1948 the 'Big Four' railways now became the six Regions of one body, the Railway Executive, in turn responsible to the British

Below:
'Business as usual' in Darlington Works during World War 2. 'A8' 4-6-2T No 2162, in unlined black and with minimum lettering, is reunited with its wheels after overhaul in March 1944. The spirit of the works is still preserved today in the murals which adorn the walls of Morrison's tasteful supermarket restaurant, now occupying the site of the old works building. The clatter of cutlery and crockery helps to conjure the memories of the roar and thunder of hammers and presses which filled the building during its century of locomotive care and construction. *Ian Allan Library*

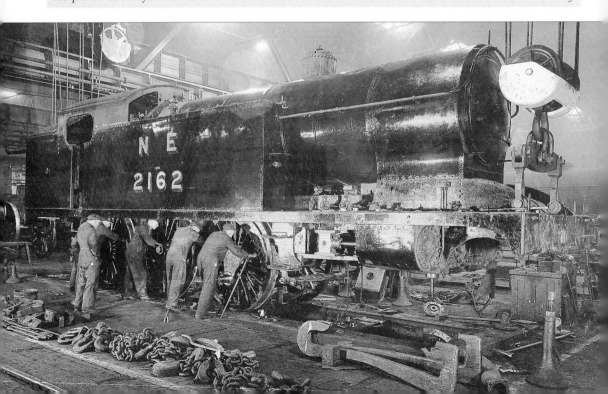

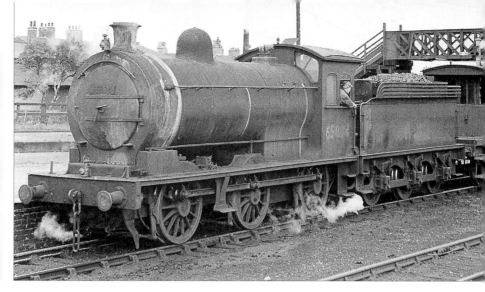

Right:
A forlorn 'J27' (NER 'P3'), No 65884 from Stockton shed, sets back through Redcar with a North Yorkshire goods in August 1951. *P H. Wells*

Above:
Middlesbrough from the southwest in 1947. The 1846 M&R line to the North Yorkshire coast is to the right of the docks nearest the camera, running from Middlesbrough locomotive shed, past Guisborough Junction and through Cargo Fleet station (Cleveland Port until 1867). At the top left, across the Tees, Bell's ironworks of 1853 still stands. *Aero Pictorial Ltd/Darlington*

Transport Commission and the Minister of Transport. The North Eastern Area of the LNER became the North Eastern Region of that plural singularity, British Railways (BR). However, a new government disbanded the Railway Executive in October 1953, placing British Railways directly under the British Transport Commission. Thus politics increased the confusion of the first years of the struggle to maintain the railways' place in a new economic world characterised by rapidly increasing and better-provided road competition. On Teesside the vast ICI company's conversion to oil power in 1951 exemplified this change and was hardly balanced by the construction of a new branch

Below:
A 'standard' Stainmore engine, 'J21' No 65097 leaves Kirkby Stephen for Darlington with the 11.5am SO Blackpool to Darlington. It would appear that more pushing than pulling is being done as the train approaches the first 1 in 72 up grade! *K. B. Green*

line to serve its Wilton works. It was such local needs which went unnoticed by the new, all-embracing experiments of the Railway Executive, and would not be scrutinised until steadily falling revenue attracted a ministerial enquiry in 1954 — about five years too late.

At Shildon, the 24 'laden' roads, once lined with North Eastern wagonloads of coal, Pease & Partners' own coke wagons, lime and limestone, Middleton roadstone, Weardale ganister and sand, local farm freight and outshopped wagons from Shildon Works, and busy with the comings and goings of train engines and the constant sorting of Shildon loco's yard pilots and the through passage of the local passenger trains, did not regain this freight traffic during the 1950s. It continued, apparently busy, as a relief 'changing loads at Shildon' route for through freight from Tyneside to the south, while the 'empties' yard was now host not only to wagons for works but also to a gradually increasing number of surplus wagons, displaced initially by the reduction in

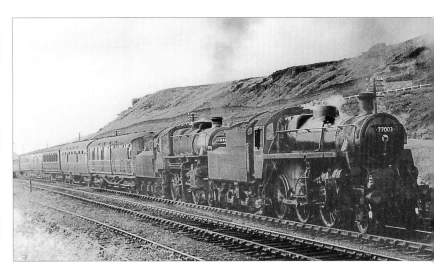

Right:
The rear of this summer
excursion demonstrates the
steepness of the gradient as
an Ivatt '4MT' is piloted
over Stainmore by one of
West Auckland's brace
of Standard Class 3 2-6-0s,
No 77003. This and No 77004
worked the last train from
Penrith to Darlington on
Saturday 20 January 1962,
running out of breath and
losing 60 minutes in the
process! *G. W. Morrison/
Darlington*

traffic and then by the new operating
requirements of modernisation.

Further out, in Teesside's 'Wild West' in 1950,
the rugged Stainmore line still carried the busy
two-way trans-Pennine mineral traffic, along
with a thriving local freight and through
passenger service which provided Pennine and
Teesdale hill-farmers with animal fodder and
trips to town respectively. Weight restrictions
meant that all these trains were worked over the
route's formidable banks by two classes of gallant
North Eastern six-wheelers with an average age
of 56. In 1955, engineers' inspection allowed the
weight limit to be raised and brought in a mix of
LMS locomotives and their new BR 'Standard'
cousins, which seemed to suggest that all was
well with Britain's highest main line railway.

But this local and increasingly typical illusion
was a further reflection of an image which was
fast becoming the symbol for all of British
Railways, an image which emerged from the
masking shadows of two world wars, an image
of falling receipts and rising costs which the first
confused years of nationalisation did little to
alleviate, and which led at last to ministerial
enquiry and the publication of the BR
Modernisation Plan.

The Railway Modernisation Plan of 1955
recognised that 'British Railways today are [sic]
not working at full efficiency' and aimed 'to
produce a thoroughly modern system' (Bonavia).
Of the five points drawn up to demonstrate the
methods which would achieve this Utopia the
most important to the freight-oriented Teesside

railways was surely Point 4, that 'Freight services
must be drastically remodelled. Continuous
brakes will be fitted to all freight wagons . . .
marshalling yards will be re-sited and modernised.'

As we have seen, in 1955 changing industry
and road competition had already begun to
remodel freight services on Teesside, while
marshalling facilities at the two major points of
local freight concentration had been constantly
rationalised to meet changes in traffic needs.

In 1952, passenger service withdrawals
between Spennymoor and Stockton, Ferryhill
and Hartlepool, and Wellfield and Murton
heralded the forthcoming economies — while
freight trains still simmered in procession,
'on the block', between Ferryhill and Teesside
hauled by trusty steamers from Newport and
Middlesbrough, Haverton Hill and Stockton
MPDs. These depots were closed in 1958,
however, and their still-ample allocations
centred on a new depot at Thornaby.

This optimistic new construction, together
with track layout changes and the installation of
colour-light signalling throughout, were the first
moves in Teesside's contribution to the
Modernisation Plan, Point 4: Tees Yard. Even
with marked reductions in traffic, such a busy
area must have a focal freight concentration
point and Newport was the obvious choice.
Thornaby shed, on the old Up Mineral Hump
site, still stands (currently host to a collection of
dead diesels) in the southwest corner of this 200-
acre yard complex which was rebuilt north and
east on the old 'Erimus' site next to the Tees.

Above:
These Teesside stalwarts moved into the new Thornaby motive power depot in 1958. In this view it must be a weekday as 'J26' No 65730, previously of Newport, and 'Q6' No 63346, ex-Middlesbrough, have Thornaby inspection pits to themselves and the maintenance staff have plenty of room to keep the new depot clean. The shed's 20th-century construction is evident. *K. Hoole/N. Stead collection*

Below:
Teesside six-wheelers stand together outside Thornaby. Again, on the left, the shed's 20th-century construction is in stark contrast to the traditional Victorian engine shed. *K. Hoole/N. Stead collection*

When the years of modernisation confusion presented the BTC with a deficit increasing from £16.5 million in 1956 to £42 million in 1959, Ernest Marples, the Minister of Transport, repeated the 'remedy' of 1953 and disbanded the BTC. Now a new British Railways Board was directly answerable to his Ministry of Transport and Sir Brian Robertson, the last commander of a railway dedicated to public service, retired in 1961. In 1963, Dr Richard Beeching, a former ICI director and the first chairman of the BRB, issued his report, *The Reshaping of British Railways*, which pointed Britain's railways, inevitably, towards the modern world of business, marketing and profit before people.

Tees Yard was officially opened in May 1963, a monument to the prosperous Erimus days and a typical example of modern miscalculation in that the forthcoming traffic reductions, decided in that very same year, were not foreseen and daily wagon numbers handled were hardly ever more than half the planned capacity. This Tees Yard optimism on the eve of Dr Beeching's remedy may be compared to the Modernisation year optimism on the Stainmore line, which was finally closed in January 1962, just five months before its centenary, after some seven years of impractical timetabling and unnecessary expenditure. The story of the systematic 'murder' of this railway has been dealt with in sober, eye-witness detail by Allan Stobbs in his book *Memories of the LNER: Southwest Durham*.

The construction of Tees high-capacity yard coincided, again typically, with the closure of the 1885 mineral lines on the quadrupled section between Stillington North and Carlton (Redmarshall since 1923) junctions. They were quickly filled with parked surplus wagons overflowing from Shildon 'empties' yard. In 1963, however, rapidly increasing road construction emphasised Britain's new prosperity and dependence on the private car when those once so busy Clarence mineral lines were finally lifted for road development. The surplus wagons were moved either into the redundant North Stockton Yard or else on to the remains of the old Clarence line which was also closed in 1963 between Simpasture and Stillington by reason of subsidence and the more urgent needs of the A1(M). After 130 years, traffic between Shildon and Teesside reverted to the original 'long' S&DR route.

Dr Beeching's report of 1963 became the axe of 1965, when railways throughout the land were cut and curtailed in the name of profit. In the North East, however, Beeching's strict medicine made little difference to the slow attrition which old age and new technology

Below:
Newport Yard in 1961 was being rebuilt into the ambitious new Tees Yard, completed in May 1963 but never to realise its full potential.
BR/Darlington

had brought to the heavy industries of the 18th and 19th centuries. In the coal industry, the first feeder of North Eastern railways, the initial rationalisation of pits turned to closure during the 1960s, and with pit closures came more railway closures.

The Castle Eden branch was also occasionally used as a wagon park during the 1950s and '60s; but only on the down (northbound) side. At these times only up, loaded, traffic used the branch while down empties climbed the banks via West Hartlepool and Hesleden. It was closed completely between Redmarshall and Wingate South in July 1966. Wingate's Colliery, of which the original branch from the HD&R had formed the foundation of the controversial GNE, C&HJR and the nucleus of a complex junction completed by the advent of the Castle Eden branch 40 years later, had closed in 1962, but in 1966, a short branch was retained from Wingate/Station Town to serve Trimdon Grange Colliery, the last

of four Trimdon collieries. Trimdon Grange pit closed in 1968 and the last piece of the GNE, C&HJR was closed in April 1969.

Meanwhile, through traffic between Bowesfield and Redmarshall (Carlton) ceased in 1967, thus ending the life of the branch which brought such welcome ease to Teesside congestion in the halcyon 1870s.

Teesside — indeed North Eastern — steam haulage also ceased in September 1967; withdrawals included the last three faithful old Raven NER 'T2' (LNER/BR 'Q6') 0-8-0s, Nos 63344 and 63387, from West Hartlepool shed, and No 63395, the last Wearside steam locomotive, from Sunderland which also resigned its last 'P2s'/'P3s' (LNER/BR 'J26s'/'J27s').

The demise of the Durham coalfield, accompanied by rationalisation of the Teesside iron and steel industry, has resulted in a much simplified layout at Bowesfield Junction, although the area of control exercised by old Bowesfield signalbox's modern interior extends to Eaglescliffe, Hartburn Junction and the remains of the layout around Stockton station. Gone are the once impressive signal gantries at Bowesfield, replaced by colour-light signals during the 1950s, but, happily, the original Bowesfield box still stands and continues its traditional role as controller of the 'western gangway' to Teesside to this day.

The old Clarence 'bough' from Teesside to Ferryhill via Sedgefield is still extant and very well kept; it makes a useful alternative route

Below:
In 1966, London Midland '4MT' 2-6-0 No 43057 of Middlesbrough coasts down to Hart Junction tender-first off Hesleden Bank on the 1835 HD&R line, with coal from the dwindling Durham field. The great variety of steam locomotion had now all but gone and the 12.00 Newcastle to Colchester coming off the direct 1905 coast line from Sunderland is powered by a completely different locomotive, English Electric Type 4 (Class 40) diesel-electric No D343. *John H. Bird*

Above:
In 1948, no fewer than 758 heavy freight engines were purchased from the Ministry of Supply for British Railways. Twenty-five were 2-10-0s and worked in Scotland; the rest were 2-8-0s and worked nearly everywhere. The 'WD' (War Department) or 'Austerity' class was the first BR Standard locomotive type and worked until the end, alongside the more traditional survivors. Two stalwarts, Nos 90076 and 90360, stand pensively outside West Hartlepool shed during the last month of steam in August 1967.
P. Cotterell

Left:
The original 1825 Darlington station stood east of the present austere 1842 building at North Road. Nowadays, North Road not only serves Bishop Auckland to Saltburn trains but also houses the Darlington Railway Centre & Museum and the Ken Hoole Study Centre. It stands opposite the 1825 works site where, 175 years on, a Peppercorn 'A1' Pacific, No 60163 *Tornado,* is under construction — the first new main line 'post-destruction' steam locomotive to be built in Great Britain. *M. Hall*

when work or 'technical difficulties' or nature closes the East Coast main line or the Hartlepool coast road. It is still regularly traversed by modern bulk freight trains hauled by ghostly Class 66 diesels, strangely silent — and featureless — after the clank and roar of 'Ps' and 'Ts', while the old S&DR line between Middlesbrough and Darlington, although not running precisely on its original course, has outlived all. The cross-country 'Sprinters' and local 'Pacers' give little idea, as they sweep silently — and characterlessly — through often deserted Bowesfield Junction or else beneath a screaming jetliner as it drops into Teesside Airport, of what it was like to travel the line behind *Globe*, or even those big old, yet remembered 'H1' and 'D' 4-4-4 / 4-6-2 tanks! Today's units join the GNER Class 91 electrics, descendants of Sir Vincent Raven's unlucky No 13, at Polam Junction on the old S&DR Croft branch into Darlington where you may still see *Locomotion* and some of her successors resting in the North Road station museum. From Darlington you may travel on to old Shildon, where, thankfully, the genius of Timothy Hackworth is eternally remembered in the publicity of his own home, and then on to the Aucklands — where it all began.

Left:
No 1275 is an original S&DR '1001' class 0-6-0 seen in 1975 shortly after arrival at Darlington North Road station where she waits, permanently, in the museum platform. Behind stands No 1463, the first of the 'Tennant' NER top-link passenger class designed by a team in 1884 after McDonnell's resignation. Their 'back to Fletcher basics' success can be attributed in the main to Wilson Worsdell — some five years before he became CME. With *Locomotion* and *Derwent* they stand as permanent memorials to Britain's unique Industrial Revolution, and to the first public railway which served it, the old Stockton & Darlington whose Northern Spirit still survives on the world's first passenger route.
D. L. Percival

On Teesside Routes

EAST OF TEESSIDE
— Saltburn–Middlesbrough —

Right:
The massive proportions of the North Eastern Pacific tank show to advantage in this shot of 'A8' No 69894 as it runs round at Saltburn terminus, its home station, in 1956.
P. B. Booth/N. Stead collection

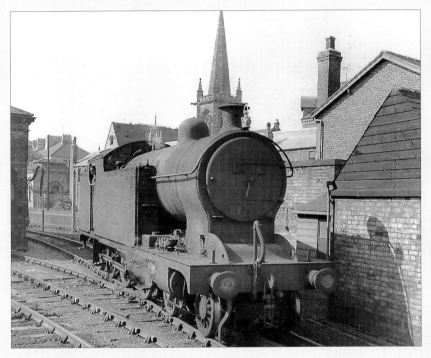

Below:
Marske station looking towards Saltburn. Marske was the only intermediate stop on the Saltburn extension until 1929 when Redcar East was opened.
R. Coulthard/N. Stead collection

Right:
'A5' 4-6-2T No 69831 gets away nicely from Redcar with a train for Saltburn in August 1951. Gresley had these Great Central-type Pacific tanks built for the North Yorkshire coast line in 1925 when the adhesion of the 'D' 4-4-4Ts proved inadequate. They worked until the end alongside the NER 'A8' conversions and the new, postwar Thompson LNER 'L1' 2-6-4Ts. *P. H. Wells*

Below:
'A8' No 69869 is homeward bound at Redcar Central with a Saltburn train in June 1954. *L. A. Strudwick*

MIDDLESBROUGH
— Teesside Hub —

Top right:
In 1842 a goods spur was built from the S&DR's Middlesbrough branch to serve the new dock. The spur left the branch at Old Town Junction. In 1846 the Redcar extension left the spur at Dock Hill Junction. Middlesbrough's passenger station was then isolated from the new main line and a new station built on the present site. Considerable increase in traffic resulted in the 1877 rebuild into the imposing edifice seen here at the turn of the 19th century. *Darlington*

Right
Teesside's docks received more than their share of enemy bomber attention during World War 2 and a hit on Middlesbrough station in August 1942 unfortunately laid bare the lofty skeleton of its roof which led to a further rebuild. *Ian Allan Library*

Lower right:
'A8' No 69826 stands in Middlesbrough station with a Yorkshire coast train in BR days. The remains of the 1877 roof, retained after the 1942 bombing, are visible at the far end. *Darlington*

ROUND TEESSIDE
— Newport–Darlington —

Right:
The crew keep a sharp look behind as 'J26' 0-6-0 No 65743 forges eagerly through Newport Yard, past the locomotive depot, with an inter-yard transfer trip and no brake van. *R. E. Vincent*

Below:
In 1950, 'T1' (NER 'X') 4-8-0T No 69910 shunts Newport No 1 Up Hump Yard. *P. W. B. Semmens*

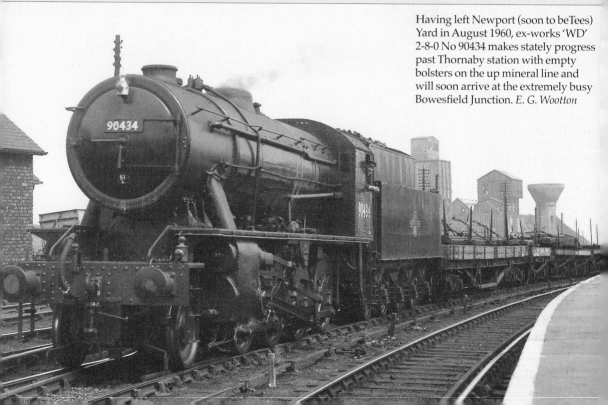

Having left Newport (soon to be Tees) Yard in August 1960, ex-works 'WD' 2-8-0 No 90434 makes stately progress past Thornaby station with empty bolsters on the up mineral line and will soon arrive at the extremely busy Bowesfield Junction. *E. G. Wootton*

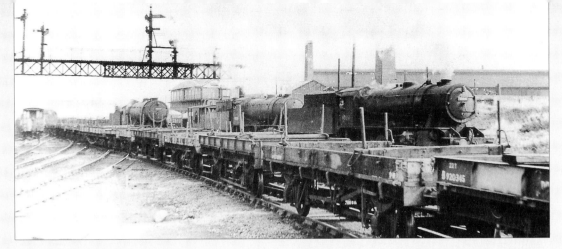

Above:
Bowesfield Junction is fully occupied in this 1958 scene; the train nearest Bowesfield box is 'super-powered' by two 'WDs' and is on the up main line heading for Eaglescliffe. The down main is unoccupied, while another 'WD', beyond the gantry, is either bound for Carlton Junction or waiting to cross on to the LN Stockton/Hartlepool lines on the left, when the train of down empty bolsters from Carlton has cleared.
Darlington

Left:
Saturday 27 September 1958 and Bowesfield is completely empty! The main line to the right will soon cross the Tees on the 1841 bridge to Thornaby, Middlesbrough and the East Coast. In the middle distance is the entry to Newport Yard — Tees Yard from 1963. The line in the distance (extreme left) led round to the S&DR's — and the world's — first passenger terminus near St John's Crossing.
Darlington

Left:
The line from Bowesfield to Carlton Junction soon crosses the Leeds Northern main line, just south of Hartburn Junction, partly hidden here by Hartlepool-based 'WD' No 90588's eruption as it heads south on the LN in fine style with mineral empties. The 2-8-0 will join the main line from Bowesfield at Eaglescliffe.
John M. Boyes

Above:
'WD' No 90517 of Newport steams well through Eaglescliffe with freight for Teesside via the old Leeds Northern line on 25 March 1961. The S&DR lines, moved closer to the LNR in 1853, are nearest the camera.
P. B. Booth/N. Stead collection

Right:
Darlington terminators usually ran into one of Bank Top's two separated bays. In July 1954, neat 'J72' No 69022's lamps announce the important post of station pilot as it waits with a hopeful driver between the busy south-end bays. A Teesside arrival stands on the right. *Martin A. Cooper*

Left:
At the 'stops' end of the same road an 'L1' contemplates its venerable ancestor, *Locomotion*, which stood on a plinth here with Hackworth's *Derwent* (on the left) for many years.
R. E. Vincent

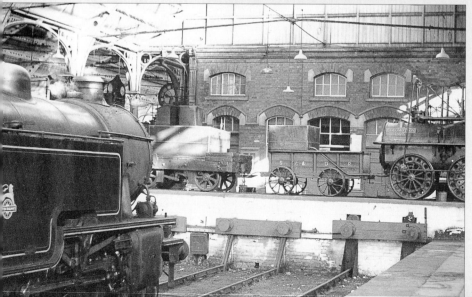

Left:
Bank Top station was built in 1887 west of the original lines which became through-running roads outside the station building. The exit beyond the bays takes you out to the 'bank top' of Victoria Road, directly opposite the dignified clock tower. This view was taken from Park Lane. The quickest way into the Peases' busy yet peaceful town is usually to *walk* down the 'bank'. *LGRP*

Viewed from Parkgate bridge exit at the north end of the station on 22 February 1953, 'A5' No 69835 comes up across the layout to the down side with a connecting service from Ferryhill when through services were suspended due to engineering work at Aycliffe. (Engineering inconvenience is not a 21st century invention!) *R. E. Vincent*

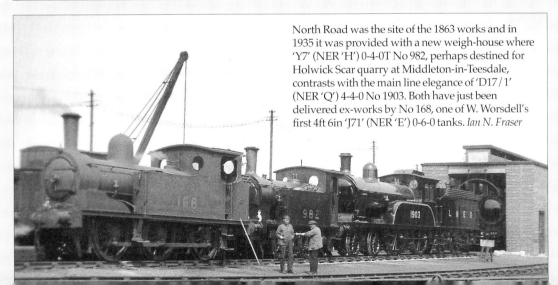

North Road was the site of the 1863 works and in 1935 it was provided with a new weigh-house where 'Y7' (NER 'H') 0-4-0T No 982, perhaps destined for Holwick Scar quarry at Middleton-in-Teesdale, contrasts with the main line elegance of 'D17/1' (NER 'Q') 4-4-0 No 1903. Both have just been delivered ex-works by No 168, one of W. Worsdell's first 4ft 6in 'J71' (NER 'E') 0-6-0 tanks. *Ian N. Fraser*

THE 'WILD WEST'
— Darlington–Kirkby Stephen–Bishop Auckland —

Above:
After Forcett Junction the Stainmore main line became single track and crossed the River Tees at Winston — as 'G5' (NER 'O') No 67305 nimbly demonstrates on a Middleton-in-Teesdale train in 1954. This was Darlington shed's 'regular' engine for Middleton and worked the last steam service on 16 September 1957. She had previously been the Ferryhill to Spennymoor regular and worked that branch's last service on 31 March 1952. Unfortunately, there were no more regular jobs for No 67305 after Middleton-in-Teesdale and she was withdrawn after a short Tyneside exile to South Blyth shed, her fame unsung! *P. W. B. Semmens*

Below:
Latter-day Stainmore sophistication: two-year-old BR Standard Class 3 2-6-2T No 82027 of Kirkby Stephen comes away from Barnard Castle, past the East 'box with a train for Darlington in December 1954. Kirkby Stephen had No 82026 as well, while Darlington had Nos '28 and '29; they replaced the sexagenarian 'J21' (NER 'C1') 0-6-0s. The nearest road, left of the 'box, led to the goods shed which started life as the first D&BCR station in 1856. *J. W. Armstrong*

Between 1930 and 1935 seven ex-GNR 'D3' 4-4-0s worked over Stainmore. Their meagre cabs upset unpredictable enginemen, just as surely as their hardy predecessors had complained about the big cabs thoughtfully provided by Bouch on the first bogie engines almost a century before! No 4347 looks uncomfortably 'Great Northern' as it waits to leave Middleton-in-Teesdale in June 1935.
H. C. Casserley/Darlington

Soon after leaving Barnard Castle westbound trains crossed Tees Viaduct, the first of several spectacular viaducts which took the line across the Pennine becks and rivers. The main line began to climb immediately at 1 in 70, while the Middleton-in-Teesdale branch turned right with the river at Tees Valley Junction, and in some 5-6 miles came to Middleton nestling in beautiful Teesdale. Here Middleton village lies across the river, hidden behind the station, while Monks Moor climbs into Middleton Common beyond. The two-mile private branch to Holwick Scar stone quarry, worked by one of T. W. Worsdell's diminutive 'H' ('Y7') 0-4-0 tank engines, continued left out of the station.
Darlington Public Library

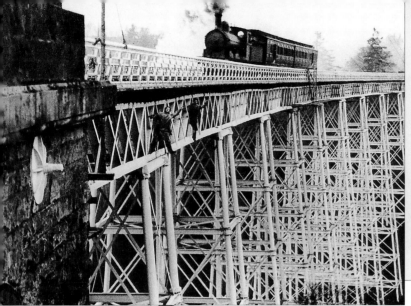

Left:
Deepdale Viaduct provided a platform for some dangerous dancing way back in 1933, with a 'C1', then but a sprightly 40-year-old on a westbound train, climbing briskly towards the turn to the east. The line then swung back round westwards, and eased through Bowes, then stiffened again towards the final three miles at 1 in 68 to Spital and the highest summit on Britain's railways at Stainmore.
Fox Photos Ltd/Darlington

Right:
One of Darlington's Standard Class 3 tanks, No 82028, drops the tablet at lonely Belah 'box on the way home on 10 March 1956 with the 10.32am from Penrith.
J. W. Armstrong

Left:
After Belah the line continued to descend at 1 in 69/72 into Kirkby Stephen's compact layout, seen here from the west with everything on show, from left to right: locomotive shed, up yard, passenger station and down yard. The gradient climbs visibly beyond as the line heads for the heights of Stainmore lowering in the distance.
B. R. Goodland/Darlington

Above:
No 78019, one of four BR Standard 'Mickey Mouse'
Class 2 2-6-0s allocated to Kirkby Stephen, makes a
fine study in the shed yard on Whit weekend 1958.
In this year the depot (51H) was transferred from the
North Eastern Region to the London Midland Region,
becoming 12E. The locomotive is today preserved on
the Great Central Railway in Leicestershire. *R. M. Lush*

Below:
In August 1947, the last year before Nationalisation,
'traditional' 0-6-0 (C1) 'J21' No 5119 strolls away from
Kirkby Stephen into the last single-track, west-by-
north lap to Eden Valley Junction and Penrith.
The other branch turned southwest to Tebay.
Ian Allan Library

Left:
Ready to leave Barnard Castle for Darlington in 1927 is No 1477 of the well-known 1886 top-link McDonnell interregnum 'Tennant' class. They were working over Stainmore around amalgamation time as LNER Class E5 and did as well over the hills as they had done on the East Coast main line. They were replaced by the GNR 'D3s' in 1930. *J. E. Kite*

Right:
The line from Darlington comes in from the right and passes under the imposing gantry at Barnard Castle's eastern approaches. This view was taken from a train leaving for Bishop Auckland behind a 'G5' 0-4-4T in July 1954. *Darlington*

Left:
The up goods yard at Bishop Auckland was the domain of a rather unusual pilot, Sentinel 'Y3' class 4-wheel vertical boiler locomotive No 68149 of 1927. Chain-driven Sentinel shunters were usually employed in works and docks, but single-manned economy proved ideal for this small station yard. *D. Fairley*

SHILDON
— 'The Cradle of the Railways' —

Above:
From Bishop Auckland the main line south, joined the east end of the 'tunnel branch', and after the tunnel itself dropped down into Shildon, which 'J26' No 65731 of West Auckland shed has just cleared with a brake van from Auckland Yard in this 1962 view. The station is on the right, while on the left the old loco depot coal drops point the way to Timothy Hackworth's home and Soho Works, 'cradle of the railways', which finally became Shildon wagon works

and now house the Hackworth Museum. No 65731 approaches Shildon Yard (see p88).
I. S. Carr/Darlington

Below:
Shildon Works is seen here in c1870 with 1868 long-boilered 0-6-0 No 215 as background for the works staff picture. The site now forms the Hackworth Museum centred on Timothy Hackworth's own Soho Cottage. *Darlington*

Right:
It is still possible to walk the path which follows the original way to West Auckland via the Brusselton and Etherley inclines, pausing at The New Masons, now very much refurbished but still the same public house whence No 1 set out with the inaugural train in 1825. *Author*

Below:
The 'cradle of the railways' and *Royal George* memorial now marks the spot, while the nearby traffic roundabout has been utilised as a second reminder of the world's earliest steam railway. *Author*

Below:
Masons Arms crossing is seen in 'active service' in this c1895 view with the Masons Arms on the left and an NER tank approaching from Shildon. Soon after Masons Arms Shildon Works was reached before Brusselton East Incline ascended and the way can still be followed up to Brusselton Top.
K. L. Taylor/Darlington

Above:
Brusselton engine house is seen from the west incline, minus winding drums, with locals and livestock in the late 19th century. *NRM/Darlington*

Left:
The scene can still be uncannily recognised today from further down the incline; the engine house is on the right at the top, although it no longer spans the 'way' and has lost two chimney pots. *Author*

THE S&DR ROUTE

Shildon to Stockton

Right:
Stockton's present station was built in 1852 upon the arrival of the Leeds Northern Railway, heralding years of amalgamation. Here LNER Thompson 'K1' 2-6-0 No 62005 represents the last days of steam as she brings empty stock under Stockton's lofty arches for the SLS 'Three Dales' railtour on 20 May 1967. 'K1s' worked throughout the Eastern system, but No 62005 was a Darlington engine and is now happily preserved in full working order on the North Yorkshire Moors Railway. *M. Dunnett*

Below:
Shildon yards 'laden' (left) and 'empties' (right), with a diesel shunter in attendance; both are quite full in this 1960s view, as '4MT' 2-6-0 No 43129 of Darlington hurries into Shildon with a train for Bishop Auckland. *N. E. Stead/Darlington*

Below right:
The BR Modernisation Plan had already decreed the end of steam in 1959 — but we didn't believe it! Graceful Gresley 'V2' 2-6-2 No 60962 of Heaton shed heads out of Stockton towards Hartburn Junction, Eaglescliffe and the west with the 4.15pm Newcastle to Liverpool on Whit Monday, 18 May 1959. True to NER practice, goods lines pass outside the passenger station at Stockton, on the down side. *S. E. Teasdale*

ROUND TEESSIDE
— Stockton–Hartlepools —

Above:
The Leeds Northern joined the old Clarence branch at North Shore Junction in 1852 when Stockton's Clarence/S&H station was bypassed. In 1920 a new relief line branched northeast from North Shore in order to link with Haverton Hill and the industry around Port Clarence. In the 1960s No 63430 comes eagerly through North Shore Junction on the main line with coal for Tees Yard. *K. Hoole/N. Stead collection*

Below:
A 'Q6' gingerly steers a heavy load, most likely for Hartlepool, tender-first off the curve from Norton South Junction on to the old Clarence's 1833 main line at Norton East in BR days. This 1873 curve parallels the course of the much tighter S&HR 1841 original. *P. B. Booth/N. Stead collection*

Above:
The S&H/LN main line left the Clarence line just east of Billingham and soon came to Greatham, then Seaton Carew, a Teesside resort with remarkably golden sands to which families from industrial southeast Durham escaped during the golden summers of the 1950s. A variety of motive power travelled the LNR main line in LNER days. Here a fairly new 1927 Gresley Class D49 'Hunt' three-cylinder 4-4-0, designed for secondary passenger work, nears journey's end as it gallops through Greatham from Leeds. This is No 375 (later Nos 2773/62773) *The South Durham*. This LNER design, the ultimate in northern four-coupled development, worked exclusively in former NER and North British Railway territories. *Ian Allan Library*

Below:
'Q6' No 63387 steams healthily through Billingham station with an up goods from Hartlepool on 22 August 1967 in the last month of north eastern steam operations. Attrition had finally left Nos 63344 and 63387 as the last two NER engines at West Hartlepool. They were withdrawn in September with the last handful of 'WD' 'Austerity' 2-8-0s. *M. J. Fox*

Right:
'H' class Sentinel railcar No 2140 *Eagle* pulls away from Greatham on a local service. This was one of 49 six-cylinder geared steam cars built for the LNER between 1928 and 1931.
Ian Allan Library

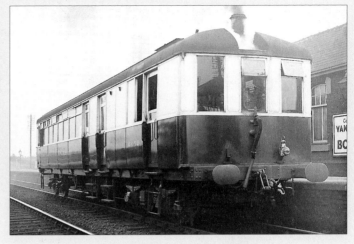

Right:
NE 'O2' (LNER 'G5' class 0-4-4T No 413 (later No 7343) is near Seaton Carew in 1937 with a local train.
R. E. Kirkbright

Below:
Top-link work was over for Wilson Worsdell's Class V Atlantics in 1937. Now, as LNER Class C6, No 697 spends a quiet day near Seaton Carew with a Teesside Sunday excursion.
R. E. Kirkbright

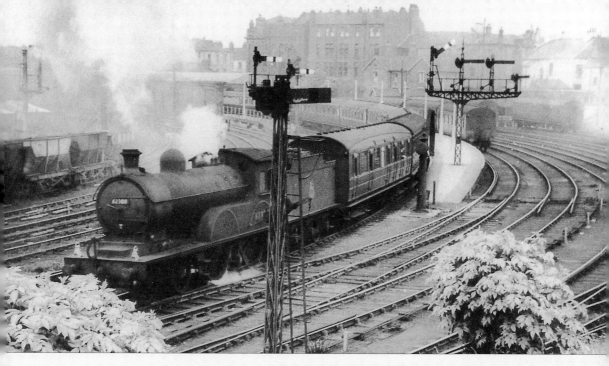

Above:
Class D20 No 62380 (NER 'R' No 1026) of 1907 was still heading Class A trains on the LN main line in early BR days. It is seen tackling West Hartlepool's curves in fine style, shortly before withdrawal in 1954. *C. R. Payne/Darlington*

Below:
No 62005 and the SLS 'Three Dales' railtour stock again. Coming round from West Hartlepool station, No 62005 heads for Stockton through Newburn Junction on 20 May 1967. The 1840 S&H line went straight into the docks behind the train, while the roads crossing the main line in the foreground went to Burn Road Goods and the once busy but now long gone works sidings. *John M. Boyes*

ROUND TEESSIDE
— Hartlepools–Ferryhill–Spennymoor —

Above:
In 1967 one of the last pair of Teesside 'Q6s', No 63387, heads coals from Hetton. Hesleden's gradient climbs beyond the bridge behind. After Hart, the 0-8-0 will reach Cemetery North Junction where the main line bears right for West Hartlepool and Teesside, away from the 1835 line into Old Hartlepool and the original HD&R docks terminus. *A. M. Bowman*

Below:
In the final year of steam, one of the last 'WD' 2-8-0s, No 90116, slinks into Hesleden up goods loop with a load of coals so that the guard can pin brakes before descent of the bank. *John M. Boyes*

Above:
No 90116 passes the remains of Wellfield station and the signalbox and approaches Castle Eden Junction. *John M. Boyes*

Left:
Coxhoe North Junction at Ferryhill was approached from the Coxhoe goods branch, the beginning and end of the old Clarence Railway's Sherburn branch of 1835. In 1961 'Q6' No 63421 was seen bringing block cement from the Portland works, by then the only goods from the Coxhoe branch. The ECML ran through on the left. *D. A. Idle*

Below left:
The Clarence's Byers Green branch continued the line from the Hartlepools westward. Leaving the industry around Ferryhill, within three miles it entered the industry around Spennymoor, with Dean & Chapter Colliery on the down side, Weardale Iron Co's coke works and foundries on the up side and sundry factories all around. To the northwest of Spennymoor, Bell Bros owned Whitworth and Page Bank collieries until 1931. These were served by the Byers Green branch, which continued westward from Spennymoor station. They were used as sidings right up to closure of the branch in 1966. All railways and industry have now gone from the area and were already declining in the early 1950s, when 'G5' No 67318 was seen with a train from Ferryhill, while 'Q6' No 63380, left, was engaged in the then still lengthy Spennymoor shunt on the goods road beyond. *W. A. Camwell*

Bibliography

Social and Economic History

Mid-Victorian Britain, 1851-1875, Best, G., Panther, 1971

The Rise of Industrial Society in England, 1815-1885, Checkland, S. S., Longman, 1964

Longman Handbook of Modern British History, 3rd edition, Cook, C. and Stevenson, J., Longman, 1996

Early Victorian Britain, Harrison, J. F. C., Fontana, 1971

The Age of Extremes, Hobsbawm, E. J., Michael Joseph, 1994

The Age of Revolution: Revolution, Capital and *Empire* (3 vols), Hobsbawm, E. J., Weidenfeld & Nicolson, 1962-87

Industry and Empire, Hobsbawm, E. J., Pelican, 1968

British Society, 1914-1945, Stevenson, J., Penguin, 1984

Railway History

Railways of England, Acworth, Sir W. M., 1889

North Eastern Railway, Allen, C. J., Ian Allan, 1964

Shildon-Newport in Retrospect, Appleby, K. C., RCTS, 1990

Castle Eden Branch, Betteny, Alan, Atkinson Pubs, W. Hartlepool, Printability Publishing Ltd, 1993

British Rail, The First 25 Years, Bonavia, M., David & Charles

History of the LNER, Bonavia, M., George Allen & Unwin, 1982

Locomotives at the Grouping 2: LNER, Casserley, H. C., and Johnston, S. W., Ian Allan, 1966

North Eastern Railway, Historical Maps, Cook, R. A., and Hoole, K., Railway & Canal Historical Society, 1975, revised 1991

Locomotion, Faith, N., BBC, 1993

Gresley Locomotives, Haresnape, Brian, Ian Allan, 1981

Northeast England: Forgotten Railways, Hoole, K., David & Charles, 1973

Railways in Cleveland, Hoole, K., Dalesman Books, 1971

A Regional History of the Railways of Great Britain: Vol 4 The Northeast , Hoole, K., David & Charles, 1965

North Eastern Railway Company, 1870-1914, Irving, R. J., Leicester University, 1976

Encyclopaedia of British Steam Locomotives, Nock, O. S., Blandford Press, 1964

Great Northern Railway, Nock, O. S., Ian Allan, 1968

Locomotives of the North Eastern Railway, Nock, O. S., Ian Allan, 1954

Chronicle of the Stockton & Darlington Railway, Proud, John H., North Eastern Railway Association, 1998

Railways in England and Wales, 1830-1914 vols, Simmons, Jack, 1978

Victorian Railways, Simmons, Jack, Thames & Hudson, 1991

Memories of the LNER: Southwest Durham, Stobbs, Allan W., 1989

North Eastern Railway, Tomlinson, W. W., 1914 (David & Charles, 3rd edition 1987)

North Eastern Steam, Tuplin, H. A., George Allen & Unwin, 1970

Railwaymen, Politics and Money, Vaughan, Adrian, John Murray, 1997

Railways of Great Britain & Ireland, Whishaw, Francis, 1842 (David & Charles, 1969)

Timothy Hackworth and the Locomotive, Young, R., Shildon, 1923 (Stockton & Darlington Jubilee Committee, 1975)

Local History

Brewster's Stockton, 1829 [Brewster 1753-1842]

A Place Called Teesside: A Locality in a Global Economy , Beynon, H., Hudson, R., Sadler, D., Edinburgh University Press for the University of Durham, 1994

Coal Mining in County Durham, Durham County Environmental Study Group, 1993

Teesside at Mid-Century, An Industrial and Economic Survey, House, J. W., Fullerton, B., Macmillan, 1960

Story of Cleveland, Horton, Minnie C., Cleveland Libraries, 1979

Trimdon Snippets, Johnson, Eveline Roberts, Printability Publishers with Sedgefield Borough Council, 1998

History of Middlesbrough, Lillie, W., Middlesbrough Corporation, 1968

Teesside's Economic Heritage, North, G. A., Cleveland County Council, 1975

Middlesbrough Town and Community 1830-1950, Pollard, A. J., ed., Sutton Publishers in association with Middlesbrough Borough and the University of Teesside, 1996

Collieries of Durham (2 vols), Temple, Index Books, LDN, 1994

Jackson's Town, Waggett, E., Hartlepool Borough Council, 1979

Memories of Ferryhill, Wall, G. D., County Durham Books DCC Arts, Libraries, Museums, 1994

Magazine Articles

Locomotives Illustrated, Nos 120 (1996), 123 (1999); 132 (2000)

Steam Days, 'The Spennymoor Branch', Ryder, Colin, May 2000